T0144033

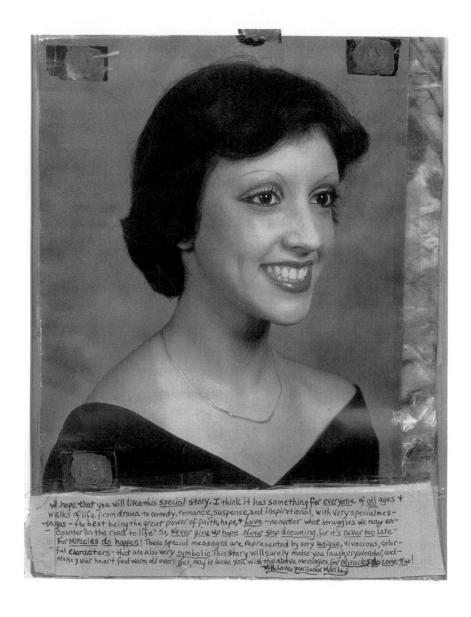

I hope that you will like this special story. I think it has something for everyone of all ages & walks of life. From drama to comedy, romance, suspense, and inspirational, with very special messages - the best being the great power of faith, hope, & Love - no matter what struggles we may encounter on the road to life." So, Never give up hope. Never stop dreaming, for it's never too late" For Miracles do happen! These special messages are represented by very unique, vivacious, colorful characters - that are also very symbolic. This story will surely make you laugh, cry, wonder, and make your heart feel warm all over! Yet, may it leave you with the above messages, for Miracles do come true!
With Love, your author, Marilu

To order additional copies of this book, contact:
Xlibris
1-888-795-4274
www.Xlibris.com
Orders@Xlibris.com

A Bit About The Author/Illustrator

Fashion design by "Marilu"

Maria Luisa Robles (Nickname: "Marilu"),Author and Illustrator of *The Magic Wheels of Love.*

Born: September 25 in Manhattan, New York Education: Bishop Denis J. O'Connell and J.E.B. Stuart High Schools, graduated with four year Honor Roll Northern Virginia Community College, Nova Community College, A.A. and A.S. (magna cum laude—each) Concentrations: Psychology, Education and Languages, Charter Oak State College; completed B.A. (with concentrations listed below under "special studies") Special Studies: Psychology Education, and Foreign Languages (Spanish and French), English, Language Studies and Writing: I am trying to complete my Master's degree in Psychology and help others from a distance on a 24/7 basis, as mentioned later. Held Occupations: College student, translator, tutor, writer, language teacher (Spanish, French, English T.E.S.L.) Social Worker, T.E.S.I. director/coordinator. Also, although I am presently quite ill with severe Fibromyalgia and other painful muscoskeletal illness, I am now trying to complete a Masters Degree in Psychology by distance learning on a 24/7 basis, as mentioned above, to help others as a –Dear Abbey, writing advice to newspapers, magazines, etc. and/or set up my own website like "Dear Abbey"—and to teach bilingually from a distance on a 24/7 basis Psychology, and perhaps also languages.Memberships Held: International Society of Authors and Artists, International Club and the French Honor Society, Glee Club and Catholic Church choir and youth group, Catholic Writers Group. I am now quite ill yet, I hope to belong to Writers' groups as above, if able to and affordable again Other

Published Works: Poetry – "A love That True" (Yet, I retain a copyright of this, as I was told). Awards Received: Merit of Outstanding Literacy Achievement, "A Love that's True." Scholarly Certificate Awards for best student of graduating class in Social Studies and Foreign Language (French), Excellence in Spanish Catholic War Veterans Award for Best Student of Graduating Class in Social Studies. Graduated from High School with 4-year Honor Roll and Magna Cum Laude for College. Also received a diploma in Biblical counseling from the American Association of Christian Counselors. Personal Comments: "Born in New York City of Cuban parents, and of Spanish descent, I'm completely bilingual in English, Spanish, linguistically and culturally. Besides my studies in Psychology. Foreign Languages and English, I've also formally studied classical ballet and dance for 10 years. I've taught Spanish, French and English as a second language for many years at all age levels, including work as a volunteer. I enjoy helping others. Since I've become ill, with more time alone, I've created and written a special fiction novel, and a collection of poems and lyrics and some foreign versions, which I hope to publish. Also, being ill and alone with my only "earth-angel," my Mom, yet economically poor-like-me, the publication of my creative work could help to "save" my Mom and my life to survive economically, and, if published, with your help, would also donate a part of my profits to help others; through charity, as I promised, and hopefully help others who read my novel by leaving a very special message of love and hope, so needed today and always; and to "never give up" on your dreams, because dreams can come true. It's never "too late" because "miracles do happen!"

Lovingly,
Your Author,
"Marilu"

Accomplishment Of Merit

This certifies that the Board of Judges has noted

MARIA L. ROBLES

for the outstanding literary achievement entitled

"A LOVE THAT'S TRUE"

Charles J. Palmer
Charles J. Palmer
Editor-In-Chief, Creative Arts & Science Enterprises

BCC

Annual Membership Certificate

The International Society Of Authors and Artists

Certifies that

Maria Luisa Robles

is a distinguished member

with all the rights and privileges thereof

during the membership year.

Charles J. Palmer
Charles J. Palmer
Chairman

This is another award I won for poetry, which I created and wrote, andthis poem was nominated for world peace alongside with other poets suchas our former President Clinton and other important world leaders andcreative advocates for world peace. This poem was also published for non-profit and for which i retain full copyright. The name of this poem iscalled "Let's teach the Children"©

"Remmembering "Happy Days" as a dancerYour Author as a"Dancing Flapper" in a masquerade party, to the right with a look alike "Elvis" and a"Japanese lady" in happy friendship sharing and dancing days."

"Me as a "20's Dancing Flapper" with an "Elvis-look-a-like" and a "Japanese lady" at a charity Holloween party."

"Me at "Bee-Bop 50's" happy dancing days."

"An (my) elegant "Sweet Sixteen Celebration", dancing first with my godfather in waltz."

Dedication

I lovingly dedicate this book to my "two" mothers ~ The Blessed Virgin Mary ~ Mother of god and her divine son in the 2nd trinity ~ Jesus Christ – "who sent me" – my only "earth angel" – to be there fore me through good times and ill times ~ especially since I became very ill with fibromyalgia (severe) and other spinal and muscoskeletal painful illnesses – supporting me as my illness progressed in every kind and loving way as only a mother could do – sent from "Heaven" ~ for me ~ Hortensia Robles – may mother and to the rest of my "sacred family" in Heaven ~ St. Joseph ~ The Blessed Mother of god's patient and kind husband ~ and a wonderful father to the Lord Jesus in his earthly – existence – being divine also; yet showing us the "way the, truth and the light" and all other angels and saints "my spiritual heavenly family," and again to my "earth-angel" mom – who has been – my only source – besides the heavenly – of support, encouragement, love, kindness, dedication to me, since I was born and especially when such a severe illness progressed – the only "angel" who has been there for me through the pain, and who taught me through he loving example to me of a selfless kind and giving life – never to give up on my dreams, regardless of what others may say ~ or think, and to <u>never</u> give up <u>hope</u> – that with "our sacred heavenly family" has also showed me – the same and that "<u>miracles can happen</u>" – no matter how difficult this may seem. And, to St. Jude, the patron saint "impossible" – so called – "cases." For "<u>there is nothing impossible with God.</u>" I dedicate this to all who suffer pain of any kind and their loved ones, also – so that the messages in my novel with its–<u>symbolic</u> – <u>characters</u> will inspire you and fill you with <u>faith</u>, <u>hope</u> and <u>love</u> – Always and to "<u>Never – give up on your dreams</u>"–if they are good – <u>for it is never too late! With God All is Possible.</u>

Lovingly your author, "Marilu"

"Marilu"

THE MAGIC WHEELS

OF LOVE ©

Created and Written
By
Maria Luisa Robles, 1996 ©

"Magic" can come in many ways. Most of all thru "Love" (your author, as a "Jeannie")

Chapter One

There once was a boy named Jesse. He lived with his dad who was a young widower. Jesse's mom died when he was a little baby so he only knows his mom through photographs and what his dad has shared with him of memories. Jesse is a very nice young boy; however, Jesse became ill recently and he can no longer walk. He uses a wheelchair to get around, but it's a bit old and worn out so they must get him a new one. This, however, is a bit of a problem since Jesse's dad's business has not been doing too well lately. It is a home care business he runs out of his own home since he is a carpenter and a bit of a mechanical and engineering wiz. He studied mechanical engineering for a few, years until he had to leave college to care for his family and help out when his dad died. Yet with his knowledge and know-how for building things and good head for business, he set up his own business of home and auto care and repair. It was doing very well too—until recently when things have been going too slow. This was very bad since Jesse's dad could take care of Jesse more working out of his home. This might mean that now his dad would have to go and look for a job and spend less time with Jesse. Also, it was harder for him to compete with others who did graduate from college. Yet, they were now economically poor and Jesse needed a new wheelchair.

It hasn't been a good year for Jesse. He too had to miss a lot of school and many other activities as well. He can no longer play and run like he used to. His muscles have become weaker. This illness has weakened his frail little body. Josef-that's Jesse's dad's name—was very sad, especially when he thought of the idea of having to leave Jesse all day to go to work for somebody else. And, whom would he be able to leave Jesse with during that time? Yet he thought to himself. "No, I must go out and find a job soon if business does not get better. I can't wait too long since Jesse needs a new wheelchair, especially if I can't manage to fix this one up." This made Josef very sad and angry at the same time, especially since he was so good at fixing things. After all, he could build a house being a carpenter and even build a car with his mechanical engineering know-how and formal education background. On that subject, would anyone even give him a job with so many other college graduates competing out there for one? Would he have a fair chance at one? All of this worried Josef a lot. Yet, he had to at least try if his home business did not get better soon. He became angry thinking why is it that I just can't seem to fix Jesse's wheelchair when I've rebuilt engines and more? He just couldn't understand this. So of course, he felt quite discouraged.

Jesse and Josef were very close. They had a great relationship. Not only were they father and son, they were also best friends. Jesse could tell when Josef was feeling sad even though Josef tried to hide his sad feelings from Jesse many times, so that Jesse would not worry. Yet, Jesse did worry about his dad when he saw him worry no matter how hard Josef tried to hide this from Jesse. Jesse knew. He could tell when his dad was troubled, and he wasn't going to let him suffer alone. He wanted to help or at least try. So, after a while of trying to find out what was wrong, Josef realized that hiding his feelings from Jesse was only worrying Jesse even more. Josef sat down beside Jesse and explained to him in a way that wouldn't scare Jesse. Jesse wasn't too afraid of feeling scared though. With all that he has been through, he could understand this feeling and could sense it pretty much in others too. Jesse was a very kind and sensitive boy; he cared about other people's feelings. After his dad explained that he might have to leave home during the day and possibly work elsewhere, Jesse understood, and he told his dad not to worry that he was going to be all right no matter what, although he admitted that he was going to miss his dad. His dad hugged him and told him that he was going to miss him too. After all, Jesse spent most of the day with Josef especially while Josef worked in his workshop, which he built at the backside of the house. Jesse used to love watching his dad work and the smell of the wood and everything. Josef had set up a little space for Jesse too with a bed and a great color TV that he had placed safely in a place where both of them could see it. Jesse especially loved to watch the car races on TV.

Jesse used to dream of being a hot rod race car driver despite the risks involved. Sadly, it seemed that Josef would-not have to worry about that now. Yet, they enjoyed watching TV together.

Jesse loved the workshop. He had a great big window up beside his bed. He used to love to see the big oak tree in the background change colors from summer green to fall orange and yellow and red to snowy white and then to beautiful colors and flowers all around it during the spring again. He especially, loved to see the stars shine bright at night. This was a special place for Jesse and Josef as they shared many good times here. They always managed to find some time to have a good laugh, as Jesse's dad would tell him some jokes at times. Yes, this was a very special place for both of them. If Josef could not fix Jesse's chair soon they sure would miss spending so much time there together when Josef would have to go out to work elsewhere.

Well, after many trials, Josef still couldn't get the chair fixed. He decided that he was going to at least try to sell the parts and, hopefully, get some money for them to help save for a new chair for Jesse. Josef decided to take it apart the next day. It had been a long day for him. Jesse had fallen asleep in his little bed in the workshop and Josef did not have the heart to wake him up. So he opened the door which led to the living room and decided to rest on the couch in the living room where he could keep an eye on Jesse until Jesse woke up. He then planned to carry him up to his bedroom in the house and put him to sleep there. Josef started to read trying to keep awake until then. Yet, he just couldn't keep awake; it had been a very long day and he had stayed up later trying to fix Jesse's chair that night. He fell asleep on the couch in the living room.

Meanwhile, Jesse was asleep in the workshop. The workshop was all dark except for the moonlight's rays shining in Jesse's window and a dim night light plus the light shadows which came in from the living room light where Josef had fallen asleep. Poor Josef was so tired that even the light he had kept on in the living room to help prevent him from falling asleep could not keep him awake. All was quiet as the bright star in the sky shone upon this peaceful home. Yet, there was a sense that something magical was about to happen.

Chapter Two

Jesse had been asleep in the workshop ever since his big eyes closed while watching the car races earlier. As much as he didn't want to miss—the race, he was so tired that he just fell asleep. Yet, in his dreams all sure was not quiet. Jesse was having a wonderful dream in which he was a famous race car driver. In his dream his car was a bright shiny red color, and he had on a bright white uniform with red-line trims. His race number was '7'—his favorite number. He was in this long flashing red race car, and he was driving ahead of all of the other cars in the race all the way.

Even though Jesse was driving fast in the race, he could see all of the things and places that he passed through. He saw beautiful big trees and flowers and in the middle of it all he found himself on top of a huge long bridge with the blue ocean and sky all around it. Fishes and seashells of all colors jumped up to greet him as he passed by. Even the palm trees waved their palms in greeting to him. They all wished Jesse great luck and cheered him on as he passed by.

Jesse felt great with the wind rushing past his face and the sea breeze he so loved to smell. Then he found himself at the end of the bridge in a beautiful town filled with lots of beautiful trees, flowers, and animals like horses that also cheered him on. Then right before he came to the finish line, all of the people on the side of the road also cheered him on as he began to cross the finish line.

Jesse was so happy when all of a sudden he was awakened as the real wind came rushing from outside into the workshop window above his head as the sound of the real tress played their tune against the sound of the wind. Then, all of a sudden, Jesse heard a strange voice say to him: Jesse . . . Jesse, wake up. Don't be afraid. Everything is okay. I'm going to be your friend. My name is Rodney," said the strange yet friendly voice. Jesse looked around the dark room. He thought to himself, Could I be still asleep and dreaming?"

The voice said, "Over here, Jesse—look over here by the TV stand." Jesse couldn't believe what he was seeing. There it was flowing in the dark—the wheelchair that his dad was trying to fix for him. It had big black eyes and a big smile. Now Jesse thought, "I must be dreaming or could it be I'm going crazy?" Then "Rodney" said to Jesse, "No Jesse, you're not dreaming and you're not going crazy either. I'm for real and I am talking to you. This is a real voice that you are hearing. 'I am not just a wheelchair.' I'm alive. My name is Rodney and I'm hoping to be your friend, your best friend I hope. You see, I need a friend too . . . yes, I know what you're thinking. 'But you're just a wheelchair, how can you need a friend?' But I do Jesse, just like you. See, I know that you can't walk and that is how I came into the picture and into your life. And if you let me, Jesse, I can be your friend and take you to lots of places and we can have a lot of fun together along the way. I can give you lots of 'rides.' I want to be your 'wheels' you know. Stick wit' me pal, we're gonna do lots of things, see lots of places and have lots of fun. You'll see, life's going to be an 'Adventure.' We can help each other."

Jesse looked at Rodney sadly and moved his head downward thinking, "How can I help anyone?" Rodney read his thought and told Jesse, "Don't look sad Jesse. You can be a big help. Why . . . if it weren't for you, I would just be a 'dead chair', sitting there without any meaning or purpose with nothing to do. You've helped me to 'come to life.' That's quite a lot of help!" Then Rodney said in a jokingly friendly sort of way, "Besides, if you don't help me, your dads going to take me apart, disassemble me, and take me to the dealer to see what parts of mine he can sell. And, I don't want to end up like that in a junkyard. Then Rodney continued to talk to Jesse and told him in a more serious yet always friendly way, "I may not be the best-looking wheelchair in the world, but I am a wheelchair, and I do have feelings too. Jesse, you could help me come to life. You could help to save me. You'll be giving a new meaning and purpose to my life something good to do; so, by helping me you're helping me to stay alive, and together we can both help each other, Jesse. We can do lots of things together and meet lots of nice people too. And, if you help me to help you, and we work real hard together, I think that we could help a lot of other nice people too who also need help. I'm sure that there are a lot of nice people who need help too just like us: Together Jesse, you and I could be a team and we could help them too. It'll be great! So what do you-say . . . pal? . . . buddies?"

Jesse was just amazed at what was happening. Yet, although he was a little confused, Jesse happily said to Rodney, "Yes! Yes, Rodney, I do want to be your friend too!" Jesse was so happy. It was the first time in a very long time that Jesse had felt so happy and excited and full of hope. He felt more alive. All of a sudden, it seemed that Jesse had come to life. "Yes, we'll be great friends and I want to help you too and I want you to be a best friend to me too, besides . . . Dad. You know, even if you couldn't give me a ride or take me anywhere, I don't mind. I just want you to be my friend. 'That's enough for me! Rodney, I don't want you to ever leave me."

Rodney was so happy at what Jesse told him that he told Jesse, "Jesse, it's you and me 'champ' all the way. And Jesse, I have another surprise for you." "What's that, Rodney?" "Keep your eyes fixed looking at me . . ." And all of a sudden, Rodney did a 'wheel spin,' turned all the way around in a complete circle with his back towards Jesse now and he said to Jesse, "Pardon my turning my back to you but . . ." and there was a big number on Rodney's back that also glowed in the dark . . . yes, it was a big number '7', Jesse's favorite number. At seeing this surprise, Jesse joyfully yelled to Rodney, Rodney—number 7—it's my favorite number!" "I know,"' said Rodney. "And, I also know that you have been dreaming of being a race car driver, and that this is the number that you would put on your race car."

Jesse replied, "But you know that I can't do that now-not anymore . . ." Rodney interrupted Jesse and told him, "No Jesse, you're wrong. You may not understand it for now, but you are going to be a 'Racer' and what's more a 'winner' too. Although you are already a winner—why do you think that I call 'you 'champ'?"

Jesse said, "But how?"

Rodney replied, "Don't you worry about the details of 'how' for now, Jesse. You just `believe,' you'll see. You know Jesse, there are lots of different kinds of 'races' in life. If you try your very best, someday you are going to be a 'Racer' and you are going to be a `winner' in the races. Again, why do you think that I call you 'Champ' so much? You have already begun and will continue to prepare each day for the 'Race,' `Champ.' You'll see, Jesse, just believe. Have faith in other words. You must always have faith and believe. This is very important."

Well, Jesse didn't understand all of this right now. All that he knew was that he had a lot of hope and joy in his heart at all that was happening and especially at hearing Rodney's words. With each word that Rodney spoke, Jesse felt more hope, joy and more 'alive.' Jesse was one very happy young boy! Then Jesse told Rodney, "Rodney, tomorrow we'll—tell Dad, so that he won't take you away. Okay?"

Rodney replied, "No, Jesse, for now you must keep a secret until I tell you that it's all right to tell anyone, even your Dad. I must tell you when and to whom you may tell of me." Then Jesse said, "But tomorrow Dad's going to take you apart and try to sell your parts at the dealer. No, I must tell him to stop him from doing this." Rodney interrupted Jesse by telling him: "Jesse, do you trust in me?" Jesse replied, "Of course!" ' Rodney said, "Okay then, don't worry about tomorrow. Everything is going to be all right. Just believe that. Just believe, Jesse."

At hearing these encouraging and peaceful words, Jesse, feeling more at ease and also very sleepy, closed his eyes and said to Rodney, "Okay, Rodney, good night." And then Jesse fell peacefully asleep. Rodney said to Jesse quietly as Jesse slept, Good night, champ." Jesse's favorite star outside of his window seemed to shine upon Jesse brighter and bigger than ever before as Jesse slept that evening.

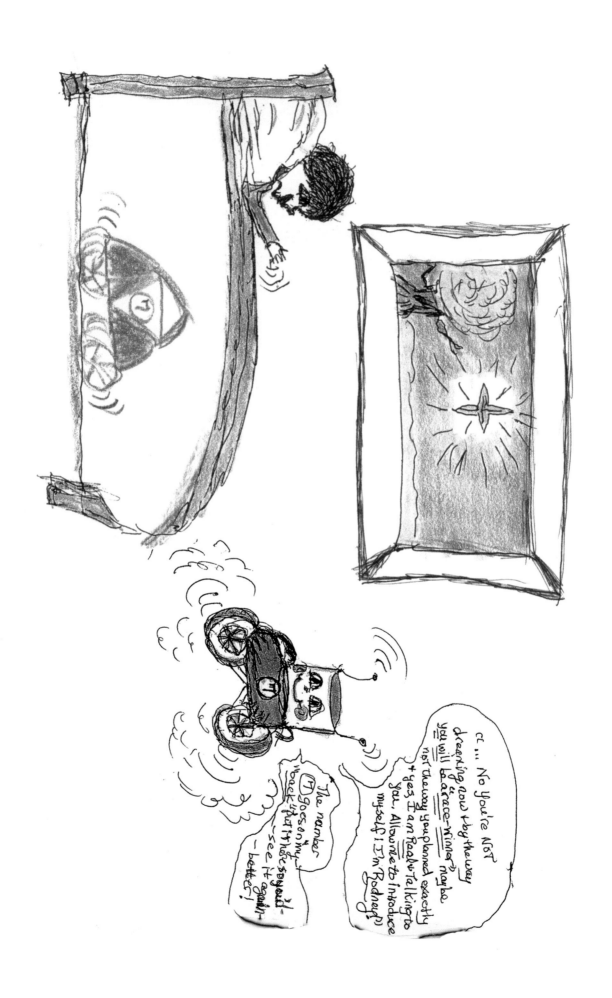

Chapter Three

Now morning came and Jesse's dad awakened still in his work clothes with the lights on in the living room, where he fell asleep last night on the couch, to supposedly keep an eye on Jesse until he woke to take him to his room to sleep. Startled. Josef rushed over to see Jesse in the workshop. Jesse was sound asleep. Josef was relieved. Then Jesse woke up and saw his dad, and he told him. "Hi Dad." Josef replied, "Hi son. Did you sleep well?" Jesse replied, "Oh yes, Dad-, great! And you?" Josef replied, "Fine son." (smiling as he thought of the situation). Then Jesse remembered Rodney and looked over to see where he was although he just looked like a regular wheelchair. Then he remembered Rodney's words of keeping all a secret. Yet Jesse waited for a sign from Rodney to tell Dad. Yet, there was no sign. So, he began to wonder if perhaps he had dreamed the whole thing. By now, he was very worried especially when Dad headed for the wheelchair that was supposed to be "'Rodney" especially when Dad said, "Well, I'll have to take this chair down to the dealer to see what parts he wants to buy, so that then I can take them apart and sell them back to him to start saving for a `real nice' wheelchair for you.

"No!" screamed Jesse. "Please don't take the chair away. Please, Dad. I love this chair. I don't want another. Please Dad!" Jesse became frantic, and Dad became worried for Jesse. So he asked him, "Son, what's the matter? It's only a wheelchair and we had already spoken about this yesterday. Remember? And you didn't get upset then." . Jesse replied, "Oh Dad, but that was yesterday. Now I do care very much! I need that wheelchair. Please Dad, I don't want another. I'll just die without it!" Josef immediately replied, "Son, don't you ever talk that way! You're my boy. L need you to live a long, long life beside me, son. You're my Pal. I love you. Please don't get upset. I'm only trying to get you the best wheelchair that I can. Trust me. I want what is best for you."

Jesse replied, "But Dad, that is the best wheelchair for me in all the world."

Josef replied, "Okay son. Don't worry. I'm only going to show the dealer the chair. If he's interested, then I'll bring the chair home again before taking apart any of its parts. And I'll do this here at home if it's all right with you. I promise, I won't do anything until I bring back the chair from the dealer and after we have a talk and agree on a solution."

Jesse, more relieved, asked Dad, "Promise Dad?" Josef replied, "Promise. Son." Then Jesse said, "Okay Dad, but please hurry back with the chair. Please Dad." Josef lovingly patted Jesse's head and told him, "Sure son. Don't worry champ. Do you feel better now?" Jesse replied, "A little, but please hurry back. Okay?" Josef replied, continuing to pat Jesse's hair, "Sure son, as soon as possible."

Then Josef carried Jesse over to the house, and they had breakfast. Although Jesse could barely eat. Later, Dad took the wheelchair over to the dealer. Jesse couldn't believe that Rodney just let him. Jesse thought to himself, "Why didn't Rodney do something to stop Dad?" Again, he dreaded the thought that maybe it was all just a beautiful dream that he had. Well, all that he could do ' was wait.

Meanwhile, Dad put "Rodney" in the loading part of the van thinking he was just driving a regular old wheelchair over to the dealer. Well after a brief trip, they had arrived. Josef took the wheelchair out of the van and took it into the dealer. He showed the wheelchair to the dealer. The dealer looked over 'the chair' and told Josef that there were a few parts that he might be interested in. Then Josef told the dealer to think about it and that there was no rush. So at the dealer's request, Josef left the wheelchair at the dealer's until tomorrow. This was so the dealer could take a good look at the chair and decide what parts he might be interested in and let him know when Josef returned to pick it up before taking it back home to talk about this to Jesse, and if agreed, work on it for those parts. Well, the dealer and Josef agreed on this and they shook hands. Then Josef left the dealer's. Yet, Josef left the wide door open when the dealer went into the other room as someone entered to speak with the dealer. As soon as this happened, "Rodney came to life," as he silently yet quickly rolled his wheels out of the wide-opened doors Josef `accidentally' left open. Rodney rolled his way out of that dealer's shop trying to catch up with and follow Josef who had already gotten into the van and had begun to leave for home. Rodney began to "trail" him by using his "magical" super laser jet-powered motor and "zoomed" his way back home. Thank goodness that it was a cloudy, foggy, and rainy day outside and not many people were outdoors as Rodney sneaked past the sidewalks, crossed the streets and tried to keep an eye on Josef on the road, and his mind on his memory of how they had gotten to the dealer so that he, could switch his memory back to `reverse' to go back home. This is how Rodney's `brain' works or one should say his `wheels' work when traveling. He was able to do this. Yet, whenever Rodney saw someone walking in or out of a place, he immediately sneaked into a side alley behind a building or some other hiding place to disappear from their sight. Poor Rodney! He did all of this the whole way home and in the rain too!

One man who had been drinking the night before and awoke to see

Rodney zooming by thought to himself, "I've gotta stop drinking! I guess I had ' one too many drinks last night and now I'm beginning to see things. A speeding rolling wheelchair with no one in it in the rain." He then promised himself that he would never drink again! Rodney being able to read his mind thought to himself joyfully, "Well, that's great. My good deed for the day!" He smiled. Well, you can imagine what happened to those who caught a glimpse of the rolling 'Hot Rod' wheelchair with no one in it! Yet, thank goodness he finally made it home. Yes, before Dad!

When" Jesse, all sad—and teary-eyed, heard the door open, he saw 'Rodney' appear. It was as if Jesse came alive again. He was so happy! Jesse yelled out to 'Rodney, "It's true, you are for real! You're not just a dream I had. You do exist, and it's really you, Rodney! It's you! And you came back! Oh Rodney, thank you!"

Then Rodney replied with a few tears of joy of his own mixed with the raindrops all over him, "Didn't I tell you to trust and believe?" Jesse, ashamed at his past doubts, looked downward and before he could say anything, Rodney smiled at Jesse and Rodney told Jesse cheeringly, "Hey champ, buddy, pal-it's you and me from now on, together all the way! I won't ever leave you Jesse. Remember, we're a team!"

Jesse then replied to Rodney, "Yes Rodney, we are a team for-always!"

Now they heard Jesse's dad pull up the driveway: Jesse looked at Rodney thinking, "what should he do?" Rodney, reading Jesse's mind, replied to him, "Don't worry, Jesse. Remember: trust and believe." Jesse replied, "Okay, Rodney, I will."

Dad came in to the workshop at home where Jesse was and said, "Hello Jesse, I'm home!" He then began to tell Jesse of his trip to the dealer's when all of a sudden, he turned around and saw the wheelchair-soaking wet sitting there. "It couldn't be," he said to himself. "I just left it at the dealer's-dry." Then he thought, "I must be seeing things!" Then he told Jesse, "Jesse, I'm afraid that I'm not feeling too well. I better go and lie down for awhile, but I have to call the dealer first. He'll think that I brought the chair back and he'll think that I am crazy. Oh, Jesse, what will I do?"

Jesse looked at Rodney and Rodney nodded to Jesse that it was all right for him to finally introduce him to Dad. So, Jesse reassured Dad that he was not crazy and that everything was all right. Jesse told his dad, "Dad, sit down, please. We need to talk. The reason why I did not want for you to take the wheelchair you built for me away is because this is no ordinary wheelchair. This is sort of a `magical' wheelchair. I can't explain how it came to be. It just is. Trust me, Dad, it's, a very special and unique wheelchair. Do you believe in miracles Dad?" Dad replied to Jesse, "Why yes, of course, I think that I do. I believe in the miracles of the Bible and in those that continue to happen." "I also believe in them, Dad. Thanks to what you've taught me and I learned in religion class. Dad, do you believe what they say, that God works in mysterious ways?" Dad responded to Jesse, "Well son, yes, I do believe that." He looked at the wet wheelchair again and added, "I better believe that!"

Jesse laughed lovingly and told Dad, "No, Dad, you're not going crazy! What you see is for real. This wheelchair is . . . yes . . . it's a miracle. I cannot think of another word for it that could ever describe it so well."

Then Dad said to Jesse, "Please tell me more about this miracle, son." Jesse said, "It's a long story, but I will explain."

Then Jesse told Dad the entire story of what happened the night before when he met Rodney and of their conversation then. After Jesse finished the story, Dad understood and he told Jesse, "No wonder that you did not want me to take it away. Now I understand the look of joy on your face. Yet, well . . . I guess that 'Rodney only talks to nice young boys like you, son. That's okay as long as he makes you happy, I'm happy too. It—I mean Rodney—must hate me for having taken him to the dealer. I wonder how he got back home."

At hearing this, Rodney spoke to Dad and said, "Sir, if I may introduce myself my name is Rodney. I'm Jesse's friend and I hope to be yours too, if you'd like."

Dad was astounded. Rodney noticed and continued to tell him, "But sir, I'll admit, you sure had me spinning and turning as I tried to follow you home. You sure have a lot of winding streets, roads, and alleys in this town. It's not exactly like 'singing in the rain' getting back home! Yet, miracles do happen and here I am."

Meanwhile, Dad was still amazed yet reassured by Jesse's peace, joy, and faith, which were quite contagious to him—he smiled. Then, he looked downward working at trying to hide the tear in his eye. He then looked at Rodney and again at Jesse and this time bowed his head in his hands and softly said, "Dear Lord, Thank You for bringing Jesse and me such a wonderful miracle. Thank You for Your love for us. Thank You so much my sweet Lord." Jesse and Rodney close by heard his words and were filled with love and joy. Then, still with a tear of joy in his eye and a heart full of love, Dad lifted his head after he finished saying his prayer and he looked at Jesse again and lovingly smiled and then turned to Rodney and with a huge smile told him, "Rodney, welcome to our family."

Dad then dried up Rodney and brought him over to Jesse's side and then carried Jesse and sat him on Rodney. Then Dad embraced both Jesse and Rodney with the warmest most loving hug that one could imagine and he said, "Thank you Lord for sending us Rodney. Thank you Lord, for You have blessed us with a miracle."

Chapter Four

Well, it was now after Jesse's latest visit to the doctor. Jesse was told that he must continue to remain in bed and at home for a long time still. This was, of course, difficult for Jesse. Yes, Dad and Rodney saw to it that Jesse's spirits were kept up. They read together, watched TV, played checkers and some video games, and laughed at Dad's jokes and some of Rodney's too. Yes, they made the best of it. They also went to church for Sunday Mass every week together. It was there that they saw Jesse's favorite school teacher, Ms. Mary Francis, who was also very fond of Jesse. She, was very concerned about Jesse and about the possibility of his falling behind in school; so, when Jesse introduced her and Dad, she proposed the idea of her tutoring Jesse at home. Jesse's dad was not able to pay her yet for this, as he began to explain to her, when Ms. Francis interrupted him by saying: "Please, Mr. Rosel, don't. misunderstand-I wish to volunteer for this, if you don't mind. See, my little girl is also ill and has missed some school days herself. Since I tutor her everyday and they are in the same grade, I could tutor Jesse at the same time. It would be good for both of them I believe. Besides, Jesse's too bright to have him falling behind. He has great potential. So what do you say? Is it all right with you?"

Overcome with her kindness, Josef responded: "It's just great. I am so grateful. I was worried about Jesse falling behind in his schoolwork, yet being so busy with my work and everything and not being able to afford a private tutor for Jesse, well you can imagine . . ." "No need to worry: I'm just glad for the opportunity to help out a little."

Then the priest came over to greet them and he stayed talking with Jesse while Josef and Ms. Francis stepped aside for a bit to talk more. "You see, I understand. My little girl is also confined to her wheelchair due to an accident. She had a bad fall and has had to be in her chair ever since. The doctors say that an operation is quite risky and give her a fifty-fifty chance. So, we are trying to investigate other options, including physical therapy. You see, she was studying very hard to become a ballerina. She was quite good too. Yet now, well, we don't know if she'll ever be able to walk again much less dance."

As she said this, her eyes watered and her voice sort of choked. Jesse's dad knowing all too well the feeling tried to comfort and cheer her a bit. "Now Ms. Francis, I understand how you feel. It is very painful for one as the parent to see your child full of dreams, and well . . . and to cry. Yet let's never lose faith. Let's never stop dreaming or lose hope. After all, thank God, miracles have a strange way of happening and even surprising us at times. Please, believe that. It will be okay, you'll see."

Then, he gave her his handkerchief and she shyly apologized for her slight display of emotions. Then Josef interrupted her and said in a cheerful way, "Now, now. What's this Mr. Rosel business? Josef s the name, at least to all of my friends. I hope that you'll do me the honor of being one of them." . "Only if you call me Mary Fran, That's what my friends call me." They both smiled and shook hands. As she began to give Josef back his handkerchief, Josef put it back in her hand. "Please Mary Fran, keep it as a souvenir of what I told you and just remember, whenever you feel like you might need a handkerchief again. And if you, ever feel like, you need a shoulder to lean on well, you just call on me please. That's what friends are for." "Thank you Josef. It helps me to know and the same goes for you." "Thank you, Mary Fran. I'll remember that too."

This was good for Mary Fran. She was a young widow too. It was good for Josef too to have a new friend. They went back now to join Jesse and Rodney, of course, and Father who was making Jesse laugh as he told him one of his jokes. So they all agreed that it was a great idea for Ms. Francis to tutor Jesse and her little girl at the same time. They agreed that next Tuesday night would be a good date for this and set the time for 7:00 PM.

So at 7:00 PM Tuesday night, Ms. Francis and her little girl, Francie went over to Jesse's house for their first lesson together. It seemed that Jesse and Francie had known each other from school. They were in one of their classes together. Although they didn't know each other very well, they used to sit close, by in one of their classes in school before. Jesse remembered how pretty she always was and Francie how cute Jesse was. Yes, it seems that they secretly had a small crush on each other since then. So, when their parents introduced them, they both blushed shyly and smiled cutely at each other.

"Well it seems that you two have already met. That's great!" the two parents agreed. Then, it was time for Josef and Mary Francis to discuss the lesson plans for the week. While they did this, they let Jesse and Francie wait for them in the family room. Here Jesse and Francie waited while watching TV. Of course, Rodney was 'silently' there too, acting just like a normal ordinary wheelchair, as he did whenever he was not alone with Jesse and Josef. All of a sudden, a beautiful ballerina began to dance ballet on the TV program that they were watching. Francie's eyes lit up, just like Jesse's did whenever he watched a car race on TV. Yet soon, Francie's eyes started to water and by the time the commercial came on, there were tears rolling down her big brown eyes. Jesse noticed this.

"Francie, what's the matter? Why are you crying?" Jesse looked concerned. "I'm sorry. It's just that I always dreamed of becoming a ballerina. I was doing well in my classes too, until I fell and now I'll never be able to dance again."

Now Jesse's eyes began to water too. So did Rodney's although Francie couldn't see him. So, Rodney spoke to Jesse in a way that only Jesse could hear. "Jesse, we've got to do something. We can't let that nice little girl stay so sad and give up hope or her dreams." Jesse thought, "Yes, but what can we do?" Rodney, reading Jesse's mind said, "I know . . . you just follow my lead and I'll tell you what to do. I am going to let Francie meet me."

Of course, only Jesse could hear Rodney. Jesse smiled when Rodney told him this. He did as Rodney said. Rodney told Jesse to repeat to Francie what he was going to be telling Jesse to tell to Francie. Jesse agreed "in thought." So, Jesse began to tell Francie what Rodney instructed him to say. "Francie, don't cry," Jesse began. "I know it's hard and it seems as though your dreams may not come true, but somehow, some way, they will. Maybe a little differently than you imagined them to be, yet, they will come true. You'll see."

Francie replied, "But how Jesse? I wanted to be a ballerina, and I can't even walk now. How can I ever dance? How could I ever be a ballerina?" So, she cried even more now.

All of a sudden, Rodney turned out all of the lights in the family room and he turned Jesse around—and the back side of the chair or 'Rodney' glowed in—the dark. See, whenever Jesse's back was not resting on the chair, Rodney's face was there; but whenever Jesse's back was resting on the chair, then Rodney's face switched over to the back side of the back of the chair—behind Jesse's back. Rodney turned Jesse around in the chair so that Francie could see his face—now on Jesse's back side of the chair—and Rodney's face glowed in the dark, with his eyes bright and his smile big, smiling at Francie. Rodney then spoke to Francie: "Don't be afraid, Francie, I'm Rodney, Jesse's friend and wheelchair. Yes, I talk, but only to those whom I choose and especially to those who I want to be my friends. If you let me, I'd like to be your friend, Francie."

Francie was astounded. As she looked at Rodney's big smile glowing in the dark, with her tears still flowing down her cheek, she just kept looking at Rodney not believing her eyes. She then spoke to Jesse and said: "Jesse, is this a trick of yours? . . . I'm scared!" Rodney then told Francie: "No, Francie, this is no trick. I'm for real!" Jesse told Francie: "Yes, Francie, it's true. I couldn't believe it either when I first met Rodney. Believe me he's for real. It's really true! I have a very special 'wheelchair.' Rodney is-'for real' and he is really my friend. I used to be sad, like you are now. Oh, I still have my moments. It's not easy. I understand how you feel. Yet, ever since I met Rodney I feel really happy inside, you know. It's hard to explain, but ever since I met Rodney I have more hope and joy. just can't explain it. It's . . . well, it's like a miracle. It is a miracle! Rodney is a miracle. He has helped me to believe that no matter what happens, I can still be happy, and life is good and worth living. It can be an 'adventure', even in our wheelchairs. He helped me to believe that 'life is a miracle.' After all, they do happen. You're looking at one now!"

Francie still overcome with the emotion from it all, looked on silently and was filled with amazement.

Then Rodney created some beautiful pink and blue and golden spotlights that went around the entire room—around Jesse and Francie like in a disco. 'Rodney told Jesse to ask Francie to dance with him.—As Jesse looked at him in confusion, Rodney told Jesse: "Well, what are you waiting for?" Jesse thought: "But, we can't." Rodney, reading his thoughts, told Jesse, so only Jesse could hear him:. "Just do what I say. Ask her to dance with you." Jesse was still confused, but he knew Rodney, so he followed his lead as he was asked to do. He asked Francie very nervously, not knowing what was going to happen: "Francie, please don't think that I'm crazy and. don't be angry with me at what I'm going to ask you, please . . . but, will you . . . would you, uh . . . um, da—da—da—dance with me? I mean, if we could," he added rapidly.

Before Francie could reply, Rodney spoke and said: "But you can, Jesse, and you too, Francie! It may be a bit different than you used to before. You might call it a 'new kind of dance', but, first of all, you both must trust in me, and believe a little. Do you? Are you at least willing to try?"

Francie, all of a sudden, felt a warm feeling inside her heart. She felt so happy and warm inside. That warm feeling seemed to dry her tears away. They were all gone. Feeling all happy and warm inside, Francie smiled. She looked at Rodney and said: "Yes, Rodney, I believe, and I do trust you."

Rodney blushed, and, happy to have a new friend, smiled back at her. Then, he told Jesse and Francie: "Okay, kids, get ready."

All of a sudden Francie's wheelchair glowed in the dark too, and on her back—the back side of her chair—glowed two beautiful, big, purple eyes with big, curly eyelashes, two rosy cheeks, and a pretty, big smile with dimples to match. (Francie had two cute dimples when she smiled too!) There was a big mirror, which Rodney turned into a 3-way mirror, so Francie could see her back—the backside of her wheelchair where this new glowing face was. Then, Rodney spun Francie and her wheelchair around, so Francie could meet her own wheelchair friend who had suddenly come to life. Her name was 'Slippers', like ballet slippers. Rodney, glowing with joy, said to Francie and Jesse: "Kids, allow me to introduce our new friend, 'Slippers'."

Both Jesse and Francie were amazed! They were so surprised! Slippers winked her eye and said in a sweet and sassy voice: "Hi there, sweeties, so pleased to meet you all."

Francie and Jesse smiled at each other in amazement at it all! Then, Rodney said to Slippers: "Hello there, beautiful; would you like to dance with me?" Slippers replied: "But of course: handsome, my pleasure."

Rodney then created a beautiful chain of roses and hearts that he spun , around both his arms (Jesse's wheelchair arms) and Slippers' arms (Francie's wheelchair's aims), and the remainder of the four long strands of pink roses and hearts flew over and crossed over to each others' arms (all 4!). And where the long pink strings or strands of hearts and roses crossed together, a big knot of roses formed, tying the strings of, hearts and roses together in the center with one big heart made of roses in the center of the knot. It was a beautiful sight to see! ! !

Now, with these beautiful long strings of roses and hearts that crossed over and extended to, and connected both wheelchairs with Francie and Jesse in them, Rodney lifted his end of the string and spun Slippers around. Slippers did a beautiful spin all the way around to the sound of beautiful music that was playing in the background. Francie was filled with joy as she felt herself spinning to the music with Slippers.

Rodney and Slippers, with of course, Jesse and Francie inside, continued to spin and twirl around going forward and backward and around in a circle, dancing to the beautiful music, connected by their chains of strings of beautiful pink roses and hearts which connected at the ends with these strings wrapped around the arms of both wheelchairs. Then both Rodney and Slippers created and connected two more chains or strings of hearts and roses for Jesse and Francie to hold which wrapped around each of their wrists in a beautiful small knot with a small heart shaped of roses around each wrist like the big one in the center that connected long strands and the wheelchairs. This way Jesse and Francie could also hold on to the strings of hearts and roses that connected them, and also help to twirl and .spin themselves with Rodney and Slippers. They held on to their strings of hearts and roses as they twirled and spun around in a circle. At the same time these strings of hearts and roses moved in a circle, they also glowed in the dark. The pink, blue, and golden lights on the ceiling and walls also glowed in the dark and moved around them. Always in the center of the circle was the big, beautiful glowing pink heart made of roses on the knot that tied the strings that crossed over together. and it also spun around in a circle as the strings moved. It was a sight.

Francie happily told Jesse: "Look, Jesse, we're dancing! We're really dancing in our wheelchairs. I can feel the music like when I used to dance ballet in my ballet slippers, even more so! This is a wonderful way to dance! Do you feel the music, Jesse? Do you feel the same way?"

Jesse, not having been much of a dancer before, was amazed himself. He told Francie: "Believe it or not, I do too! I love this! This is great!"

Jesse and Francie, and Rodney and Slippers continued to spin and twirl with their magical chains of strings of hearts and roses to the tune of the beautiful song in their own "Magic Wheels of Love."

Then, at the end of the song Rodney popped a beautiful pink rose into Jesse's hand for him to give to Francie. Jesse gave the rose to Francie, and she blushed as she accepted it, thanking him. Then Rodney gave Jesse a pink rosebud attached to an elastic band for Francie to place on Slippers, which she did by .placing it on Slippers' arm. Slippers blushed and thanked Rodney too.

Then Rodney asked Francie: "Do you feel better now, Francie?"

Francie replied: "I've never felt so happy in all of my life! And, I never felt the music as alive as I did when I danced tonight. And, I've never had such wonderful ballet `slippers' either" (referring teasingly and lovingly to `Slippers'). Slippers smiled and blushed as she smelled her beautiful pink rose. Francie then put her arms around. Slippers! arms, hugging them, and then-looked at Jesse and Rodney and said: "I've never felt this happy before! I love you all! Thank you!" Then Slippers, Rodney, and Jesse all said to Francie: "We love you too, Francie!"

Yes, this was a happy foursome indeed.

Later, when Jesse's dad and Francie's mom returned, Rodney turned off the music, spotlights, and TV screen where Jesse and Francie could see themselves and Rodney and Slippers while they were dancing, and he made everything disappear except for the rosebud bracelet on slippers and the rose in Francie's hand from Jesse. Now, the glowing faces of Rodney and Slippers magically disappeared so that everything would go back to normal by the time , that Jesse and Francie's parents entered the room. Yet, before this, Francie, fearing that she had lost Slippers, began to worry. Then Slippers whispered to Francie:

"Don't worry, Francie, I am still here, and I will always be with you for as long as you wish."

Francie smiled, for she was now both happy and relieved. The TV screen flipped back to normal programming, and the normal house lights were back on now.

Then both parents walked in the family room and teasingly asked Jesse and Francie: "Did you two miss us too much? So, have you two been having a nice time watching TV and talking?" Jesse and Francie smiled at each other. Then Francie said: "Oh, yes, we've been having a `whirl of a time.'" Then, Francie's mom said: "Oh, how's that, honey?" Francie responded: "We saw the most beautiful dance on TV. It was the prettiest ballet ever!" .

Francie's mom could not believe her ears. Francie used to always cry at the mention of the word ballet or dance ever since her accident. She had never seen Francie this happy. So she asked Francie: "Oh, honey, I'm glad. I guess that means you were all right?" (she sort of asked) Francie responded, smiling in a very happy way: "Oh! I've never felt so well, Mom!"

By now, Jesse's dad suspected that Rodney had something to do with this. So, he smiled at Jesse and Jesse smiled back at Dad, nodding his head affirmatively, as if confirming his dad's suspicions.

Only Ms. Francis was completely unaware of what was happening. Then she noticed the roses on Francie's chair and on her lap. She asked Francie: "Oh, honey, where did you get such lovely roses?"

Then, Jesse in an attempt to help Francie out, without giving away their secret, responded for Francie: "Oh, Ms. Francis, I'm glad you like them. I gave them to Francie." Francie agreed with Jesse: "Yes, Mom, Jesse gave them to me." Ms. Francis thanked Jesse and said: "Oh my, Jesse, thank you for giving Francie such lovely roses. They're lovely! My, I'll bet you were surprised, huh Francie?!"

Francie replied: "You bet, Mom. I was `really' surprised!" Jesse and Francie smiled at each other. Jesse's dad was now sure that Rodney had done this, and smiled at both Jesse and Francie.

Ms. Francis thanked Jesse's dad also, thinking that he had bought the roses for Jesse to give to Francie.

Since it had taken Ms. Francis and Josef so long to discuss the lesson plans for the children, coincidentally (or not!), she decided to call it a night for tonight. She and Francie said goodnight and left, thanking Jesse and Josef again. Yet, as they left, Slippers winked `Goodbye", and Rodney blushed and winked back. Josef was surprised, yet not as much, now that he knew Rodney! Of .course, Ms. Francis did not see any of this.

So, Jesse explained everything to Dad after Ms. Francis, Slippers, and Francie left. Meanwhile, outside the house, Ms. Francis told Francie: "Oh, honey, I'm so glad that you're so happy!" Then she smiled and gave Francie a big hug and a kiss with a tear of joy in her eyes.

Francie hugged her mom back and also gave her a kiss. Meanwhile, Slippers smiled in the `background' and was filled with joy. Then they 'all' went home. The magic of that night would fill their hearts with joy and love always.

Chapter Five

As time went on the children continued to become very close friends, so did Rodney and Slippers. Their parents also became good friends. They had a lot in common, and they were both young widows and single parents. They grew quite fond of one another. The families spent quite a lot of time together, both in and outside of the tutoring lessons. They shared many social, school, and family functions. They helped and supported one another. You might say that they began to form "a family."

Both Jesse and Francie continued to see their doctors and physical therapists regularly. They both became stronger, and were now able to go back to school again-with Rodney and Slippers, of course. Yet, they continued to have the tutoring sessions, which helped them to study better. Yet, they were now less intense and not as long and as frequent as before. The extra spare time was still shared though by the two families. They had dinner and went out quite a lot together, and had lots of fun doing so. They went to the movies, the theater, picnics, shopping and lots of outings. They also shared time at home watching movies and just enjoying each other's company. They went to Sunday Mass every Sunday together. They went to the same church. They spent holidays together and shared lots of fun activities.

Jesse and Francie had most classes together at school, and always shared their lunch periods. They truly became best friends, and so did Rodney and Slippers. Yet, Rodney and Slippers were only their secret. The rest of the school didn't know it, but they had two "new additions" to their school. . Rodney and Slippers loved going there. They also enjoyed helping Jesse and Francie in their "own study sessions." Rodney and Slippers became very good tutors. Sometimes, it seemed that they had learned more than-Jesse and Francie! Rodney and Slippers quizzed the kids often and helped prepare them for exams. They had a lot of fun studying together.

At physical therapy sessions each child experienced some pain as they began to stretch and strengthen their muscles and bodies. Yet, they each gave it all they had, and they had the help and support of their individual coaches, Rodney and Slippers, ever at their side. Jesse and Francie had different physical 'therapy sessions. Yet, they always encouraged each other. Of course, so did Rodney and Slippers as their coaches, Whenever Jesse felt he just couldn't go on, there was Rodney to give him a "pep talk" and cheer him on. Slippers did the same with Francie. They would say things like: "Come on, you can do it!" Sometimes, that's all that Jesse and Francie needed to hear.

On their own separate times, Jesse and Francie spent a lot of time with their parents also. Jesse and Rodney spent a lot of time with Dad at work and around the house. The three of them had a lot of great times together, like when Dad washed the car and would kiddingly spray some water on Jesse and Rodney and vice-versa. They all sprayed the car together. Jesse's bubble baths were always fun. As both Dad and Jesse blew some soap bubbles Rodney's way, while Dad helped Jesse with his bath and shampoo, they all laughed. Yes, daily activities were lots of fun with these three kidders. Dad joined Rodney in the coaching team when helping Jesse with his physical therapy exercises at home. They really helped Jesse a lot:

Rodney and Jesse almost always accompanied Dad in the workshop while he was at work. Jesse passed Dad some of his tools while he worked, since he enjoyed helping Dad out so much. Rodney loved to be with them. Dad joked by telling Jesse to please pass the tools, like a doctor does in an operation when asking for his instruments. Jesse would respond to Dad: "Yes, Doctor." Then they would all laugh. They laughed a lot and told stories together. Rodney had quite a few to tell himself. They also watched the car races that Jesse loved so much together on TV. They rooted and cheered together. They had a lot of fun.

Over on the other "frontier" Slippers, Francie, and Mom also shared a lot of good times together. Yet Mom still didn't know about 'Slippers'. She was still a secret to her. They would all watch TV, especially the Ballet, and dance movies. They were Francie's favorites. They also laughed and enjoyed watching romantic love stories and comedies on TV. Music usually filled the house, from. the ballet classics to the modem popular variety. Mom would spin Francie around, to the beat of the music at times, which Francie loved, of course—so did Slippers even though Mom didn't know that she was spinning her around too. As Francie's body became stronger with more physical therapy and medical treatment, the doctor felt that it was now time for Francie to try more physical responsibility. So, he gave her body a test by giving her crutches to use. After much physical therapy and hard work, it was finally time to give Francie's body some more responsibility. Yet, she still had to rely on Slippers much of the time Slippers was always at her side, crutches or no crutches. There was even some talk of an operation for Francie. Yet, this would not be right away, and there was only a possibility for this. Now, she just had to keep getting stronger before anymore talk of that happening. Yet, there was more hope of this now. This was a hopeful, yet fearful, concern for Mom. Yet, Mom only shared the hopeful side with Francie, though being careful not to raise her hopes up too high, just in case. However, Mom did share her fears with Jesse's dad. He became an even greater source of support and strength for her. Meanwhile, Jesse, Rodney, and Slippers all encouraged Francie as they cheered her on while she tried to move on those crutches. They did a lot outside, especially when the weather was just right. Jesse also became a great source of support,' strength, and hope for Francie—so did Rodney and Slippers, of course.

One evening, while alone in the room with Slippers, Francie could not fall asleep. Slippers asked her what was the matter. 'Francie told Slippers that she never wanted to be separated from her even if she could walk again, and began to cry. Slippers, with a tear in her eye, told Francie: "Francie, you and I will always be together, no matter what, in our hearts. I'll always be right there with you. You must get well, and together we can help other little girls who need help just like you have."

Then, as if Francie had read Slippers' mind, she had an idea. Francie decided that if she did get well and could walk again, she would still keep Slippers, so that together they could help other little girls who would need help. She would do this by letting Slippers stay with them until Slippers taught other .wheelchairs how to help them-just like Slippers helped Francie. They might even buy these wheelchairs before giving them to the little girls so that Slippers could teach them first, without having to separate from Francie. Yet, if she did it would only be as an inspiration-to the wheelchairs the little girls had that Francie would lend Slippers to them, not for keeps. This way they could help one little girl at a time and train new wheelchairs too to do the same. Yet, either way they would help them. If Slippers did go to spend some time living with the other little girls and their own wheelchairs, as an excuse for having two wheelchairs around, they would tell the little girls' parents that, since Francie's wheelchair had been a sort of "good luck charm" for Francie, it would kind of serve as a "good luck charm" for their little girls and their wheelchairs too to hopefully serve as a "good luck charm" to them too. The reason they would not let any little girl keep Francie's wheelchair would be so that Slippers could serve as a "good luck charm" to many little girls, one at a time. Also, they would not tell the parents of Slippers' existence or of their plan for Slippers to train the other little girls' wheelchairs to learn to help their own little girls. That was their secret, of course. It was a good plan, but it would still be awhile before they could try it. They were just preparing for the future, just in case. Now, Francie felt better and more relieved; so did Slippers as she lovingly sang to Francie guarding her as she fell asleep.

Chapter Six

Now a few years has passed. Jesse and Francie were in their early teens. He was 16 and she was 15. It was another visit to the doctor for Francie. Yet, this time he told her mom that it was finally time for Francie to have the operation if her mom consented. He believed that it was time for Francie to have the operation now, since he felt that she was now ready for it and a very good specialist was willing to work with him on the case. Yet, Francie's mom was extremely worried. She was afraid that something might go wrong and happen to Francie. The doctor tried to ease her mind, but she needed some time to consider this. He granted it, but advised her not to put it off for too long.

Although tying to keep her worries and fears about the operation from Francie, Ms. Francis was very anxious about this, so on their way home they 'stopped off at church that afternoon. It was so peaceful and calm there, and there were only a few people. Slippers and Francie sat beside Mom after she entered the pew and knelt to pray. There was a beautiful statue of the Virgin Mary holding the baby Jesus in her arms. Our Blessed Mother of Jesus' loving and gentle expression in her eyes and facial expression, so beautifully depicted in her statue, seemed to be so real to all who saw her statue that it inspired many to pray to her and Jesus. This is what Francie's mom experienced as she looked at the beautiful loving statue of Our Lady and Jesus, so she began to pray and. converse with Our Lady. She prayed to her: "Dear Virgin Mary, Mother of God, and our Mom too, please help my little girl, Francie. Please don't let anything bad happen to her if she does have the operation. I do-not know what to do or what to decide on this. I am afraid. Guide me to do what is best for Francie. Please give me a sign so that I may know what to do. Oh, Dear Lady, Heavenly Mom, please, please help me; help Francie and me. We need you so much. Keep Francie in your loving care. She is so young and she is all that I have on this earth. Without her I would not want to go on."

Then she looked at the crucifix and said: "Forgive me, Dear Blessed Mother, for you above all others know what it is like to see your child suffer, and then go on ahead before you to Heaven. I must follow in your example of unconditional love and faith, for like you said to God: 'Your Will be done.' I too should say the same, but I am so weak and afraid. Please give me the strength and the faith that I need, so that I too will do God's Will and believe and trust, since that is what is best for my Francie, and, as always, for all of us. Thank you, Mom, for I know that you are with me, and with Francie too, and I know that you will take care of her and help me to do what is best, and that whatever happens, will be for the best. Thank you, Mom, for hearing my prayer and for helping Francie and me."

After she prayed, Francie's mom felt better, as if a calming peace had descended upon her and. renewed her faith and gave her a special kind of hope and strength deep inside of her spirit. She knew that she was not alone and never would be no matter what would happen. She knew that Francie was now if the "Best of Hands" and would never be alone either: So Francie's mom dried her tears hoping that Francie had not seen them. She then turned to look at Francie, who also had been praying, by the way, as was Slippers, although Mom still didn't know about Slippers. Surprisingly enough, Francie was not so afraid, it seemed, for she too had asked Our Lady to help her mom and her, no matter what would happen, and to always be with her mom, herself, and Slippers too, and to watch over them and help them always. Slippers also had been praying. She too asked Our Lady to please keep Francie safe and well, whatever the outcome and to help Francie's mom and herself to help Francie in all that they could.

After praying, Francie's mom and Francie lit some candles, close to where the statue of Our Lady carrying Jesus as a baby was, where they had been praying. Francie lit an extra candle in Slipper's name, since Slippers secretly asked her to (without Mom hearing Slippers, of course). Then they left the church.

Afterward, they stopped off, at Jesse's house. Jesse and his dad's support was also a blessing to Francie and her mom. Of course, needless to say, Rodney and Slippers were also true blessings.

Francie's mom spoke about the issue of Francie's possible operation in the living room, while Francie did the same with Jesse in the family room, a very special place for them, for as you recall, this is where Jesse, Francie, Rodney, and Slippers became friends and `danced' their magical dance to "The Magic Wheels of Love" song, which was their favorite of course. This was a very special song for them, and, of course, a very special family room since then. They also shared many good times there. Rodney and Jesse reassured Francie and Slippers, and told them that they would also pray for them. They also told them to have faith and believe, that everything would be all right, and that no matter what, they would always be with Francie and Slippers at their side too. Comforted even more again, they (Francie and Slippers) thanked Jesse and Rodney. Then Jesse had a surprise .for Francie.

Jesse told Francie: "Come over here, Francie." Francie and Slippers .moved closer by Jesse and Rodney. Then Jesse extended his arms to Francie and gave her a big hug and told her: "Don't worry, Francie, everything is going to be all right; you'll see." Then Jesse said to Rodney: "Isn't it, Rodney?" Rodney replied: "You bet it is!"

Then Jesse nervously coughed. He was a mix of emotions: faithful, hopeful, and even a little scared. Yet, an extra very special emotion was added to the list, for he seemed to feel a special kind of feeling that seemed to come over him, one he perhaps had not truly noticed before or put aside in the back of his mind without realizing it since that day that they `danced' in the family room and met again then after he had first seen her in school before then. Yet, since they continued to be together always as 'best friends', he didn't really pay attention to or think much about anything more of any special kind of feeling other than friendship between them, since this is what Francie and he always shared for years now. Of course, Jesse loved Francie, they were 'best friends.' Yet, now this special extra feeling of love seemed to come over him, a 'more than just friends kind of feeling. He thought to himself: "Could this be love?" He looked in the mirror, where he could see Rodney, and Rodney nodded affirmatively to Jesse, reading Jesse's mind. He was telling Jesse `yes' by doing so. So, after having, hugged Francie for a little while hoping to reassure her as her `best friend', Jesse began to need some reassuring himself now too before deciding to tell Francie or—not of these new or extra special kind of feelings that he felt for her. He thought to himself: "Is this the right time to tell her of this . . . ?" Of course, Rodney, reading his thoughts, again did like before and nodded his head, affirmatively, and spoke to Jesse through their thoughts, and told Jesse: "Yes, Jesse."

Now Jesse blushed and coughed a little, and cracked his voice and stuttered at first when he began to tell this to Francie: "Fran . . . Fran . . . Fran . . . Francie . . . I, I, I have something very important I must share with you." He gazed into her eyes, and got so nervous, that he became speechless. He couldn't begin to tell her how he felt about her.

Rodney, realizing this, shook his wheels a bit, trying to give Jesse a `jump ' start'; which he truly needed. Yet, Jesse continued to stutter as he said: "Uh, Francie interrupted saying: "Jesse, what's the matter? You know that you can tell me anything. Aren't I your best friend?" Looking at Rodney, she corrected herself ``I mean, your `other' best friend." She then smiled at Rodney. Then Jesse, all a bundle of nerves, told Francie: "Yes, of course you are, but also you're not. You're not . . . uh . . . well, I mean, then again you're not."

Francie shocked and in deep sorrow, exclaimed and cried out to Jesse: "I'm not your best friend?!!!" Then she began to cry desperately, and said: "Oh, Jesse, how could you stop being my friend at a time like this, when I need you the most?!!!" Then she cried and cried continuously.

Now Rodney shook his wheels so hard that he gave Jesse a bump on the bottom of his seat, and told Jesse in thought, secretly: "Jesse, if you don't tell her now, that's not the only bump that you're going to feel!!!"

Jesse, knowing Rodney meant business and, realizing that he was right, told Rodney secretly in thought: "Okay, Rodney, you're right. I'm going to tell her. I believe that I can do it now. I feel, more calm. Thanks for the bump. I needed that!!"

Rodney, in thought secretly, told Jesse: "Okay, Jesse, now you're talking!" Jesse, now reassured, calm, and more confident, began to console poor Francie and fix the confusing mess of trouble he accidentally caused. He put his hand over her head and caressed her hair gently and lifted her chin up with his other hand. He looked her straight in her beautiful, big, teary-eyed filled, bright, brown eyes, dried the tears going down her cheeks, and said to her: "Francie, don't cry. You are too my best friend, and, not only that, you are so much more to me. You are so beautiful inside and out. I've never seen prettier, sweeter, and lovelier, big, brown eyes, which become so bright in the light and when they are happy and alive with surprise at all that is funny and good. Why they speak, Francie. They are so soft and lively and bright and just so big and beautiful with those long, curly eyelashes of yours to match: Then, that golden brown hair of yours to match, and that fair-toned little precious face with rosy cheeks and dimples to match, which is so pretty and that petite, pretty little height of yours, and I could go on and on forever . . . You're just a doll! Most of all, I love your spirit, what is inside of you, that big heart that you have with so much love inside towards those who you meet, and even those that you haven't, by your care and concern for them. Yes, Francie, you are beautiful!" He took her hand and kissed it, then he looked a her big brown eyes and told her: "Francie, I'm in love with you. You are the love of my life. I love you, Francie. I love you!" He repeated this now more confident, poised, and louder. He lovingly told her: "I love you, Francie. I never felt this way before, and I never will stop as long as I live—forever!" then, thinking that she might not feel the same way towards him, Jesse said, "Yet I understand if you don't feel the way towards me, Francie. Please don't worry if you don't. I will always be your best friend and you'll never lose my friendship—ever. I too need to be your friend. That will never change, no matter what else may happen. Please, believe me. Please, also forgive me if I should not have told you this, and now of all times to tell you . . . I must be crazy! What timing I have! Oh, Francie, I hope that you don't want to stop being my friend. Can you ever forgive me for having told you this, especially now of all times?!"

Francie, completely taken by surprise, wide-eyed, and pleasantly amazed, and filled with so much joy and love, told Jesse in a kiddingly happy way: "Forgive you, Jesse?!!! No, I never will." Now, Jesse, saddened at this reply, looked downward and immediately Francie looked at him, and now it was she who lifted his chin with her hand and told Jesse: "Jesse, the reason that I can't forgive you is because there is nothing to forgive. I feel the same way that you do. I love you too. I am also in love with you, Jesse. I'm in love with my `best friend' too!" Then, looking at Slippers and Rodney, she corrected: "Well, my `other best friend.' See, Jesse, in other words, I am in love with you too! You've made me the happiest girl in the world! I love you, Jesse! I love you! ! ! Then she blushed and smiled, realizing-her `outburst' of emotions. She also told Jesse: "Jesse, I'm so glad that you told me. Thank you!"

Jesse's eyes lit up, so did his heart. He smiled at her, feeling as happy as could be and they both gave each other a kiss and a big hug. Then, Rodney and Slippers put their arms around the happy couple and hugged each other too, forming a beautiful circle of love.

They sighed happily. Then Rodney said, out loud this time: "Oh, yes, indeed; everything is going to be all right. You can bet on this!" Slippers smiled and winked her eye, in agreement at what Rodney had just said. Yes, indeed this was a happy foursome!

Remembering, the hopes of ballet/ dancing days comes alive and those to come~ For Francine again.

In a future ~> This "dream of the future" came true.

Chapter Seven

Later that same evening after Francie, Mom, and Slippers got home, Mom kissed Francie good night and tucked her in bed. She turned out the light in Francie's room and went into the living room. She sat on a sofa thinking and worrying about what to do about the operation. As she began to feel a feeling of fear again, all of a sudden, she heard a noise. She looked towards its direction, and she couldn't believe her eyes. It was Slippers—without Francie. She had just left Francie's wheelchair in Francie's room when she put her to bed. Even Francie's crutches were not in her room. They were in the living room, since she (Mom) had been polishing them that evening herself. There was no way that Francie could have put that wheelchair there, and she wouldn't do that anyway. Fearing that something might have happened to Francie, Mom went to check on her. She found Francie sound asleep in her room. "So how did that wheelchair get there?" thought Francie's mom.

When she, returned to the living room, the wheelchair was no longer in the same place that it was when she left to go to Francie's room. She thought: "How did it move all by itself to the other side of the living room? Was I going mad?"

Slippers had moved on purpose so there would be no doubt in Francie's mom's mind about how she got there by herself and moved around by herself on her, wheels without Francie's help. Slippers finally spoke to Francie's mom, respectfully calling her Miss Francis. Slippers said to her: "Miss Francis, don't be afraid. I am Slippers, yes, a talking wheelchair. No, you're not going crazy. I really exist!" Slippers then turned out the lights and glowed in the dark for Miss Francis to see her big violet eyes and big eyelashes and rosy cheeks and smile. Then Slippers spoke to Miss Francis and said: "I am Slippers, Francie's wheelchair. Yes! I am alive! I'm for `wheel' . . . ," she said jokingly and smiled, 'just a little joke, I really meant to say for 'real'."

Now, Miss Francis really thought that she was crazy. She thought that the pressure had got to her and that she had `flipped her lid'. Then she thought: "Poor Francie, who will take care of her with me crazy and in an asylum?!"

Slippers interrupted her and told Miss Francis: "No, Miss Francis, you are not going crazy and you are not going to go to any asylum either. You are well, and Francie will have her mom safe and sound by her side. Miss Francis, do you believe in miracles? I think you do. Actually, I know that you do, because I saw you praying this afternoon at church. You are a believer. Can you try to believe that what is happening is for real? Can you try to believe in me too? Why shouldn't a miracle happen to you and Francie, no matter what shape it comes in?

You both certainly deserve one, and many, more! Can't you see and possibly take this as a sign that maybe Francie is going to be all right and that she may not need to use this wheelchair you are now seeing `empty' without Francie in it?"

Francie's mom remembered her prayer at church that afternoon and how she had asked for a sign. She was now overcome with an incredibly immense and wonderful feeling of faith and hope and even joy. She now was sure that this was a sign, the sign that she was praying for earlier that afternoon at church. She smiled at Slippers and said to her: "Slippers . . . that is your name, right?" Slippers replied: "Yes, Mom!" Francie's mom said to Slippers: "I'm not sure if I'm dreaming or if you really are alive, but, either way, I believe that you came as a sign, and that you `are' the sign that I had prayed for." Mom then pinched herself and told Slippers and herself. "No, I must be awake. Yes! Slippers—like in ballet slippers." Mom thought and continued saying, now more convinced than ever before: "Yes', Slippers, you are the sign I've been praying for! You are! Oh, Slippers, you are a miracle sent from Heaven to Francie and me, and with a name like that, it truly could be no other way!!!"

Then with love, faith, hope, peace, and joy, Francie's mom looked up to Heaven and thanked Our Blessed Lady to whom she had been praying at church, and she thanked her for the answer to her prayer for a sign. She also thanked her for sending Francie and her such a 'special' miracle.

Then Francie's mom talked to Slippers, "I wish I could tell Francie about you right now, Slippers, but I must wait until she wakes up. Oh, but I wish I didn't have to! I can't wait to tell her about you! She will be so thrilled to meet you! Or, won't you still be around until then?"

Slippers smiled and told Francie's mom: "Sit down, Miss Francis, please." Nervously, Miss Francis said to Slippers: "Oh, no . . . don't tell me, it's bad news. It can't be; you're here . . ." Slippers interrupted her and said to Francie's mom: "No, Miss Francis. Au contraire. More good news! But, brace yourself." Miss Francis replied: "Okay, shoot!" Slippers asked Miss Francis: "Are you sure that you are ready?" Francie's mom replied: "Oh, please, Slippers, I can't take the suspense anymore! Have mercy!!!" Slippers smiled at Francie's mom and put her, at ease by telling her: "Miss Francis, your daughter Francie has already met me and knows me as I am. We met a very long time ago, that first time that you took us to Jesse's house to tutor him—when you and Jesse's dad left Jesse and Francie alone in the family room while you went to discuss Jesse's lesson plans. Do you remember?" Francie's mom replied: "Oh, my God, yes! That's why when I went to get Francie to go home, she was so incredibly happy for the first time since her accident. Come to think of it . . . I think that I never ever saw her so happy, not in that `special' way. Yes, ever since that day, Francie has been especially different and happy." . . . Francie's mom then talked to God and said "Oh dear Lord, thank you! Thank you for blessing us with such a wonderful miracle! I love you so much! Thank you for loving us so very much!" Francie's' mom told Slippers: "Thank you too, Slippers." Slippers smiled at Francie's mom and came closer towards her and sat beside her and told her: "Now, would you like to have some tea and have a nice chat about some more good news, arid, if you think that you can stand it, I'll tell you about some more miracles that Francie and I have experienced, since that first night that we met?" Francie's mom told Slippers: "I can't wait, 'Girl' . . . start talking!!"

So, Slippers told Francie's mom all about the wonderful miracles that Francie and she had experienced since that night that they met, and that they met Rodney as well. She told her about how all four of them, Rodney and Jesse with Francie and herself (Slippers), had danced together the night that they all met. Slippers also told Francie's mom about all the wonderful times that the four of them had had together throughout the years. Slippers and Miss Francis were talking like two sisters or friends that were 'catching up' on a long time. They talked for hours—especially Slippers while Mom listened ecstatically, surprised and delighted with each one of Slippers' words. Then Mom gave Slippers a kiss when she said good night before she went to retire to go to her room to sleep. While she was going there, Slippers told her: "Miss Francis, please promise not to let Francie know that you know about me, until I let you-know when, okay?" Miss Francis replied: "Okay, Slippers, I promise."

The next day when Miss Francis awoke she immediately went to Francie's room to see if she was all right. There was Slippers in Francie's room as usual when she woke up. Then, Francie told Slippers in thought: "I hope that it's time;

I want to tell Mom about you. Could I, Slippers?" Slippers responded in thought to Francie: "Yes, you may, Francie. It is now time for you to do so. Go ahead!" Francie smiled and joyfully said to her mom: "Mommy, good morning! Can we talk?" Francie's mom said to her: "Of course, darling, shoot!" Mom sat beside Francie on her bed with Slippers beside them, and Francie began to tell her mom: "Mom, don't be alarmed. I have. a good surprise for you, although a bit ' unusual. So, keep an open mind, okay?" Mom replied: "Of course, dear." Francie then proceeded to tell her mom: "Well, Mom, my wheelchair is not `just' a wheelchair. She talks and she's alive. She's my best friend, besides you and Jesse." Then Francie began to tell her mom everything that Slippers had already told Mom the night before.

Now, Mom knew for sure, once again, that Slippers was a true, Heaven-sent miracle and an answer to her prayer. She looked at Slippers and smiled. Slippers read Mom's mind and smiled back nodding her head affirmatively. She now knew that there was no more doubt in Miss Francis' mind. Slippers said to Francie: "Francie, I have a surprise for you. Mom and I have already met We met last night add became very good friends while you were asleep. Surprised?!"

Francie, very surprised, joyfully responded: "I sure am surprised! And I'm so glad! Oh, how wonderful) But . . . hey . . . why didn't you stop me while I was talking so much and tell me this before, or even wake me up to have been there'?"

Slippers responded to Francie: "Now, now, young lady, you needed your rest. Also, it was the right time. Remember? I told you `at the right time those who shall meet me will."`

Francie replied to Slippers: "'Yes, Slippers, I remember. You are right." Francie told Slippers and Mom: "I'm so glad that you two finally met!"

Then Mom and Slippers told Francie at the same time: "So are we!" Then they all joyfully laughed.

Mom then carried Francie and sat her up on Slippers and then Mom hugged both Francie and Slippers. While putting her arms around Francie and Slippers; Mom said lovingly: "Here they are my two girls!' Thank God, we are a family."

Chapter Eight

Well, it was now the day and all was set for Francie's operation. Josef, Jesse, Rodney and, of course, Slippers all accompanied Francie and her mom to the hospital. They all kissed Francie and wished her well. They all told tier that they loved her very much. When it was Jesse's turn he told her, with tears in his eyes he couldn't suppress, yet trying to be strong for Francie: "Francie, don't worry, everything will be all right. Remember, no matter what happens, we all love you and will always be beside you, okay? And, remember, our prayers are with you. Also remember, Francie, that I love you and always will. I love you, Francie."

Francie, also teary-eyed, yet encouraged, strengthened, and happy at his words, told Jesse: "Jesse, thank you, and I love you, too, very much. Please, remember this always because I always will, no matter what happens." Rodney and Slippers were also teary-eyed, of course.

Mom gave Francie a big hug and kiss and, trying to be strong for Francie, dried her tears, and told her that everything was going to be just fine and that their prayers were with her. She told Francie: "I love you, baby."

Francie, realizing how sad Mom was told Slippers so Mom could hear: "Okay, Slippers, now you take good care of Mom, okay?" Slippers responded: "You bet. Francie."

So, they took Francie away to prepare her for the operation. Josef, Jesse, Rodney, and Slippers stayed with Mom all night. Then, Josef, realizing how nervous all of them were while Francie was being operated on, took Mom, Jesse, Rodney, and Slippers to the hospital chapel. "There they prayed for Francie. After a long night, the operation was finally over. Thank God, it was a success. Mom looked up to Heaven and said: "Thank you." So did Jesse, Josef, Rodney and Slippers. They hugged each other and, upon the doctor's insistence, went home to get some rest to be back in a few hours when Francie might wake up, if she did not wake up later. Mom did not want to leave, neither did Jesse or the rest of the gang, but Josef took Jesse and Rodney home to try to get some sleep. Mom stayed, however, in a small cot beside Francie's bed, although this is not usually allowed. She was there when Francie awoke and so was Slippers. They were all very happy. However, it would still be a while before she could walk on her own. She needed to continue her physical therapy to strengthen her muscles and slowly use her crutches more and still use Slippers also until she was ready to walk on her own. Well, Jesse, Josef, and Rodney rushed to the hospital in the morning and Jesse gave her a beautiful bouquet of roses in a beautiful vase with a heart on it that said: "I love you." Francie love it. They hugged and were so happy to be together again.

Francie still had to stay some time in the hospital: 'But, when she was finally released, on the way home from the hospital, they stopped at their church, where they went every Sunday and where Mom had prayed with Francie and Slippers at her side before. Mom looked at the Virgin Mary's statue carrying Jesus as a baby, and this time said a prayer of thanks. She said: "Dear Virgin Mary, blessed Mother of God, thank you so much for answering my prayers for Francie. Thank you so much Heavenly Mom for answering my prayers and for Francie's successful operation. Thank you for all of the blessings you've given us, including Slippers, another miracle. Again, thanks for everything." She then looked at Jesus' statue in the Virgin Mary's arms and said: "Thank you too, my sweet Lord." Slippers and Francie also gave their thanks. Then together Mom, ' Francie, and Slippers went towards the candles and, like before, Mom and Francie lit a candle of thanks and Francie lit an extra one for Slippers.

Meanwhile, Jesse, Josef, and Rodney were preparing a surprise welcome home party for Francie. They all celebrated joyfully together.

Chapter Nine

Francie got better and better each day. Although she still rides Slippers sometimes, she is now using her crutches more frequently, and soon after much physical therapy and medical treatment. She is now ready to walk on her own. It seemed that Slipper's and Francie's plan to help other little girls was arriving. As she often did, Francie walked to the park alongside Jesse and Rodney, who wheeled right beside her. They missed Slippers, who had to stay home now. Yet, .one day they sat near a little girl who had been crying in the park in an old raggedy wheelchair. Francie, Jesse, and Rodney went to her side to comfort her. She was all alone, since the orphanage group that she was with were all playing and running in the park. She was so sad. Francie told her that she was her age when she too was in a wheelchair, and told her her story. She told her that she was going to go visit her at the orphanage. When she got home that night, Francie 'told Mom and Slippers about little Angie. Now, Slippers and Francie looked at each other and agreed that she would be their first mission of help, but since her wheelchair was so old, they decided to let Angie ride Slippers herself, and Mom and Francie and Slippers all agreed that they wanted to adopt Angie. Now, Slippers was back in use, and they all became a new family of "4 girls"!

Chapter Ten

Time passes. Francie is now completely well, and returns to her dance lessons. To be on the safe side, though, she mixes classical ballet steps with the less strenuous modern dance steps and enters into a combination style ballet. She is so good that she is offered a scholarship to study modem ballet and dance at New York's finest dance school. This means that Jesse and Francie must be apart for about 4 years. Of course, this saddened both of them, and Rodney and Slippers too, of course. Yet, they loved Francie and encouraged her to go for it, remembering the day they all first `danced' together. Teary-eyed, they said good, bye and wished her the best. Francie promised to come back to them and to write them everyday. She told them and Jesse before leaving: "Remember, I love you and you'll be with me in my heart always. And, Jesse, I love you more than before. Please don't forget that ever."

Jesse, teary-eyed, yet being strong for her, told her: "Francie, I love you too. We all do. Remember, you are free, never feel obligated to come back. No matter what, we'll always be friends."

Francie, saddened by this, said: "Jesse, don't speak like that. You know I love you and all I want is to do my best with my God-given talent, and then to come back to you whom I will always love. That is my freedom, Jesse. I love you for always. Please remember this always."

Jesse, teary-eyed, trying to be strong to set her free, thinking it was for her best interest, just hugged her and told her: "Well, now, you be good, Francie, and write us, okay?"

Francie, missing the words she needed and wanted to hear from Jesse, yet accepting his wishes, or so she thought they were, pretended to be fine with this farewell of Jesse's and said teary-eyed: "You bet, Jesse, you too. And, Rodney, please take good care of Jesse, will ya'?"—Rodney, sad and a bit annoyed with Jesse's farewell, told Francie: "Don't you worry, Francie, `you bet' I'll take care of Jesse and make sure that he behaves and writes you for both of us, We love you, Francie." Francie hugged Rodney, too, and thanked him.

Rodney told Jesse: "Why were you so cold with Francie? She loves you so!" Jesse replied: "Oh, Rodney, she should be free to be with someone who can dance with her. I cannot even walk. I'd only be a burden. It's better for her to—think that I don't love her anymore, at least not more than friendship, so that she can really be free to fall in love with someone that she can dance with." Rodney, understanding his reasoning, yet disagreeing completely, said to Jesse: "Jesse, for a bright young man, you sure are `out of it' sometimes. Francie loves you just like you love her, wheelchair or no wheelchair, walking or not walking. Remember when we all danced for the first time and she said that she never felt happier dancing? Well, just remember that, Jesse, please . . . always. You'll see, time will tell that Francie really, loves you and she meant it-when she said it was for always. Yet, knowing how stubborn you can be, I'll let you realize this on your own. You'll see Jesse:'

Chapter Eleven

While Francie is studying dance in New York, Jesse is busy back home studying at college to become a counselor. Jesse is also very busy and enthusiastic about the work that he is doing with Rodney to help other kids `on wheels' by beginning a program called the 'Wheel Racers.' In this program they train others interested in competing in the wheelchair races. These races take place all over the country. Of course, Rodney helps Jesse to prepare for. the Annual Big Wheel Race event which he will be entering soon. Dad coaches them too. The Wheel Racers became famous and are also televised. Jesse became very active starting Wheel Racer programs in school and neighborhoods. He was going to represent his district in the upcoming big race.

Yet, Jesse was never too busy to see Francie performing on TV. Francie has also been busy realizing her lifetime dream of becoming a famous ballerina. She mixes movements from the classical to the modern forms of ballet and dance and creates a very unique and beautiful modern dance ballet. She does beautiful choreography as well. Jesse never missed a performance of hers that he could see. Francie wrote to him continuously, even though Jesse, still thinking that it was best to give her as much freedom as possible, as much as this pained him, did not write to her as much and when he did it was only on a 'friendship' basis. He kept trying to give her space to fall in love with someone else who could dance with her as, obviously; he cannot.. Yet, despite the many opportunities that she has had to do so. Francie cannot and does not want to fall in love with anyone but Jesse, despite the change in his ways towards her. She values his friendship highly and is grateful for it, although she wishes for and misses the days when they shared more. So does Jesse, but he would not let Francie know that at all cost. In fact, he even stopped writing for awhile, thinking it best for Francie. Yet, Francie, although hurt and a bit confused, still invited Jesse to all of her performances, which Jesse never missed if he was physically able to go; but, he always left right after the performance and never stayed to even greet Francie. This especially hurt her since she wanted to share this success with Jesse more than anyone. Many times he would give her a false excuse for not going to see her at the performance, when, in reality, he would go yet not use the seats Francie got for him and, using another seat, which he would pay for himself and where it would be extremely .difficult for her to see him or Rodney, of course. This was not entirely impossible, since her performances usually sold out and were packed with audiences. This was not surprising since in her choreography Francie usually told a story that would give a message of faith, hope, and love which touched the hearts of many. This was in a way her way of giving back and sharing the healing miracle that she was so blessed with. She always shared her testimony of this in her interviews and speeches that she gave remembering always the days when Mom, Slippers, and she prayed to the Blessed 'Virgin Mary and Jesus in the church back home where they used to light candles after their. prayers. She misses that

A few years passed and Francie had earned her college degree in the Fine Arts with a specialization in Dance. She received honors for her dance and choreography. She traveled quite a lot, and she felt that it was now time for her to return home where she hoped to set up a Model Dance Therapy School, where children and adults with disabilities could feel their best physically and feel better emotionally through a rehabilitative dance therapy where muscles could be strengthened and hearts enlightened. She used dance as a healing instrument, and she was well known for this. She now wished to teach more than perform, so she did her last big dance performance, for a while anyway, as she planned. This was a super event and sold out practically immediately. Afterward, the Gala Ball was going to be held in her honor and all proceeds would benefit her favorite charities and part would go to a fund for her future Dance Therapy School, which would not turn away any needy person because of lack of funds. This was a worthwhile cause, one, she-hoped to foster for all in need. Well, she gave complimentary tickets to her mom and Angie and Slippers, of course, who were always at her performances and with Francie on vacations and every chance they could, going wherever she was then. Francie also sent complimentary tickets to Jesse and Rodney and Josef to her Gala Performance and the Benefit Party afterwards, although she wasn't sure that they would be there. Well, they did go and this time Jesse decided to sit in his chosen gifted seats. After all, Dad deserved this, too. Dad and Jesse wore formal tuxedos and even Rodney was elegant with his new cushioned seat and back and head rest, and yes, even a motor to go with the leather lined black elegant upholstery. Rodney was proud of his attire, of course, yet even prouder of Jesse for finally agreeing to sit in the area where Francie chose which was beside Mom, Angie and Slippers, also upholstered in a light pink cushioned leather attire, just like she was before on the day that Francie danced with Jesse on her 'Slippers'. Mom was beautiful in her evening gown and so was Angie, now 10 years old, in her pretty pink party dress. It was a beautiful reunion for all of them, especially Mom and Dad, who had not seen each other in awhile and who realized how much they missed each other since. Rodney and Slippers, of course, were always glad to see each other. Yet, in heart and spirit, they were always together.

Francie, the Prima Ballerina, looked radiant. She was lovely. She had beautiful white and pink roses on her hair and on her beautiful costume.

When Francie danced, she seemed to come alive and when she saw Jesse and the rest of the family in their seats, she was overwhelmed with joy. When she saw Jesse. her heart beat so fast she couldn't tell which were greater—the butterflies in her stomach when first coming on stage, or her heartbeat when she saw Jesse. Jesse's eyes seemed to light up when he looked at Francie. His heart was also beating fast, more so than when racing and that was a lot! She looked so beautiful and danced as lovely. He remembered her as a little girl crying in her wheelchair and then how glad she became when she met Slippers and Rodney, and they all danced. Images of their memories passed through his mind as he lovingly and proudly watched her dancing and making her dream come true. He had a tear in his eye as he remembered and watched. He was a mix of emotions—love, glad, proud, yet sad, nostalgic and longing to be with her again, to hug her and kiss her and tell her "I love you" at least once again. Rodney had a tear in his eye too, for he knew how Jesse felt, So did Slippers. Yet, they also enjoyed watching Francie's dream come true of dancing. Mom and Dad also noticed Jesse and even Francie change, although neither expressed it. Francie danced as if it would be her first and last true performance. She asked the Lord to give her strength to dance as best she could and not to make a mistake despite her nervousness, wanting to be with Jesse so. Her prayers were answered. She danced more beautifully and gracefully than ever. There was a extra sort of magic in the air. At the end of the performance she took many bows and gratefully received the lovely bouquet of roses the children from some of her charities gave to her on the stage. She gave each one a kiss. Then she said: "Here's to those of you in Heaven and on earth who have made my dream come true. I love you and thank you. May God bless you all."

Then she took a rose from her bouquet and looked directly towards where Jesse was seated and kissed the rose and threw it to Jesse. She had a tear in her eye. So did Jesse as the crowds continued to stand and yell: "Bravo, Bravo, Encore. Encore!"

Mom and Dad, Rodney and Slippers, of course, took notice of what was happening. So, when Jesse excused himself before the next curtain call, they understood and knew that he was not going to return to his seat. He couldn't bear it anymore. he just loved her so. He thought it best to leave for both of their sakes. When the curtain opened again, Francie looked at Jesse's empty seat and realized that he had left with Rodney, another tear ran down her pretty face with a deep sinking feeling that seemed to cut through her heart. The crowd continued to applaud and salute her and yell: "Bravo, Encore!"

Yet this was her last curtain call. Mom immediately told Josef to help Jesse while she would go with Slippers and Angie to try to help Francie. They were to meet afterwards at the Gala Ball in Francie's honor. Yet despite Dad and Rodney's continual persistence and insistence to Jesse that he must go to the Gala Ball for Francie, Jesse just could not bear it and refused by telling them: "She danced like an angel and looked like one too. She deserves the best, and to be with someone who can dance with her too. I cannot but dance in my heart." Tears were streaming down his face as he said this. Dad and Rodney were teary-eyed too. Rodney almost burst. Yet, they both tried to be strong for Jesse. They tried to convince Jesse that he should go at least to greet Francie and congratulate her. Yet, they understood how he must have felt.

Then Rodney said: "Champ, can't you see that the dance in your heart is the only true and best dance of all?" Dad said: "Son, Rodney is right. Please believe this, for this is true." Then, realizing that Jesse must come to realize this for himself and respecting him enough to do so, they agreed that they would do whatever Jesse decided. Dad then went to give their apologies to Francie and Mom on behalf of Jesse for their leaving and not going to the Gala Ball. Mom and Slippers understood. Francie, teary-eyed, knew in her heart that Jesse would not return. Mom and Dad then stepped aside and agreed that they must do something to reunite Jesse and Francie. They knew for their own good, they must intervene, yet in a way that would not force either Jesse or Francie. So, they agreed to talk later and come up with a good plan to do so. Rodney and Slippers agreed to do the same. Francie was grateful and glad at her success and all that she had been blessed with. Yet, she couldn't help but feel a deep pang of pain, as if a sword was cutting through to her heart as she thought Jesse and wished that he could *be by her side. She missed him so. When she was dancing with one of her good friends to a ballad that was playing, that she had to dance to to start the party before the others could dance, when the others started to dance before the song finished, she excused herself from her friend and dance partner and, with tears from her eyes. went running to the balcony where she could be alone and cried as she said: "Jesse, Jesse . . . Why can't you see that I love you . . ." she kept on crying. Then her friend and partner went to see what had happened to her, but since he had danced in the ballet with her a lot as her partner they did become good friends and so he knew all about Jesse. He tried to console her. Yet, although she appreciated it, she could not stop her sadness. Mom came over and tried to console her. She told her to remember that miracles happen, so never to lose hope or faith and to pray like they did back home at their church before. Then she said to her: "Francie, do your best, and then trust God with the rest." This helped Francie a lot. At least now her faith and hope were restored and she was more calm. She hugged Mom and Angie and Slippers and thanked them for being at her side.

er. Meanwhile— everyone was
looking for Francie — The Guest of Honor
of The Party Inside — yet she was
~~out~~ on the Terrace crying for
Jesse. Crying out to the
wind after she made her
Gala Dance Presentation in
the photo. How she wished
it was Jesse she could be with
~~instead~~ !

Francie
          dancing
with her
dance partner +
friend at the Gala
in her honor — wishing
it was Jesse instead.
The proceeds went to
her dance therapy school—
she was hoping to start
back home. So, she had to start
44 the Gala dance Yet, see
above — how she missed Jesse so!

Chapter Twelve

Meanwhile, back home Jesse, now more than ever, threw himself into his work with Rodney in preparation for the "Big Wheel Race" which was soon here. Yet, It seemed that he was trying—to put Francie out of his mind by throwing himself more than ever into the race. Of course, this was impossible. He could not forget her if he tried. So it occurred to Rodney that a plan to reunite Jesse and Francie might just work. He rushed over to tell Dad. Then Dad rushed over to the phone to call Francie's mom who was with Francie and Angie and Slippers getting ready to bring her back home. When Mom heard the plan she jumped for joy. It was brilliant. Then, she started to tell Francie and Angie and Slippers a little of the plan. Francie was planning on not staying home too long since the pain of missing Jesse was too much for her to bear. Yet Mom was hoping that this plan would keep her there at least for awhile. It was Dad's plan to build the first Model Dance Therapy School in the hometown for Francie. With the help of donations and his own contribution, which was the labor for the building that he would donate, with the help of others of course. It was also Rodney's idea that Francie would have to be the celebrity to give out the trophy to the winner of the Big Wheel Race, believing it would be Jesse, hopefully.

It was also his plan for Jesse to be the celebrity to give Francie. a bouquet of roses at the ceremony marking the day that the ground upon which the Dance School would be built would be publicized as well. It was a perfect-plan. Of course; Francie was not told about this idea for the grounds ceremony for the school or Jesse's part in it yet. This would be a surprise for her. She was only told of her part in awarding the trophy to the Big Wheel Race, to which she agreed, hoping that it would be Jesse. Jesse would not be told who the surprise celebrity would be to give him the trophy if he should win at the Big Wheel Race. He was not told about the school or his part in it either not yet—anyway, for Francie's arrival and her part in the Big Wheel Race awards ceremony was to be a surprise. He probably couldn't concentrate on the race if he even suspected, and this could not be. After all, he must win this race if Rodney's plan was to be a success.

Meanwhile, Francie watched Jesse on his television interviews for the Big Wheel Race. She was so proud of him and Rodney for the work that they were doing. She was anxious to go to see him—them—race and hopefully win. Yet, she must be kept a secret to Jesse until after the race—win or lose. So, she did not even write to Jesse until then. However, Mom, Francie, and Angie and Slippers all sent Jesse a Good Luck wreath before the race. There was no personal note attached individually from Francie. They just signed it wishing him luck.

Well, the big day arrived. Wheel racers from all over the world were going to compete. Jesse and Rodney represented their district. It was exciting. There were millions of people watching, and it was being televised and translated into different languages. Rodney was ready with a big number 7. on his back on a big red flap—Jesse's favorite number and color. Jesse had on a red helmet with the number 7 written on it. Yes, sir, they were as ready as could be. Dad was so proud of Jesse and Rodney. He told Jesse: "See, son, you are going to race after . . all! Dreams 'do' come true. Don't you ever stop believing that—ever." Jesse smiled and nodded in agreement with Dad. Jesse and Rodney and Dad then said a prayer together for God to bless them and all of the wheel racers.

Then the race began. Mom and Francie and Slippers and Angie, keeping out of sight from Jesse, yelled and rooted and cheered for Jesse and Rodney. It was a close call sometimes for Jesse and Rodney since all of the wheel racers were so good. Yet, after a very deserving fair fight, Jesse and Rodney crossed the finish line, just like Jesse had pictured in his dream when he met Rodney that first night. Yet, this was for real. He won like in his dream, yet this time he did cross the finish line and with Rodney. It was better, than his dream. Then Rodney said to Jesse: "We did it, Champ! You won!" Jesse replied: "We did it, Rodney! 'We' won! Then, after hugging each other, Mom, Dad, Angie and Slippers, and Francie all got ready for the big surprise and prepared Francie with the trophy and medal she was to give to Jesse. Dad went to hug Jesse and congratulate Jesse (and Rodney in a secret low-toned voice):'

Then the speakers all vibrated with music and cheer filled the air. Yet, Jesse still couldn't help feeling that something, rather someone, very special was missing so he felt a sad feeling. All of a sudden the announcer said: 'And now for your surprise, Jesse, and ladies and gentlemen, the famous beautiful and graceful celebrity whom we all know and love is here with us to give Jesse Rosel our winner his trophy, medal, and prize." (The prize money was to be awarded at his will to charities, including the Wheel Racers Fund and the Dance Therapy School that Francie wanted. This was a surprise to her.) "And now, without further ado, I present our. favorite ballerina, Francie Noble." Jesse's heart pounded so hard, he wondered if he was dreaming. Then his eyes lit up as she walked toward him and he said to himself: "I must be dreaming or hallucinating. It can't be . . ." Then Rodney laughed and told Jesse so only he could hear: "No, champ, you're not dreaming. It's for real! It's Francie!"

Francie's heart was beating hard tool Then she smiled at him, dimples forming adorably, she blushed, and then she congratulated him, pinned the medal on his racing uniform, and gave him the envelope with the prize money, thanking him also for his generous donations to the charities and especially to her Dance Therapy School Foundation, gave him the trophy, and then the moment all were waiting for happened.

She gave him a kiss on the lips as the crowd applauded and cheered. They hugged, and for them it seemed that they were the only two people on earth. There was magic in the air and most of all in their hearts. Then secretly Francie said to Jesse: "You're not going to get away from me now, Jesse. I've got you, and I'm never going to let go, no matter what you say or do." Jesse said to Francie also secretly: "Francie, I can't help it. I'm selfish, but I never want you to. I've tried, but I can't let go of this feeling I have for you. It's stronger than me. I'm afraid I can't win this race. All I know is that I love you. I do! I do!" Then she silenced him with another kiss as the crowd now began to cheer both Jesse and Francie. Then Mom and Dad held hands and rejoiced at this beautiful reunion. Rodney and Slippers winked to each other across the crowds rejoicing as well. Angie clapped and cheered.

Francie told Jesse: "Please don't ever win that race you spoke of with yourself— your feeling for me—because if you do, I'll be lost . . . without you. I love you, Jesse, and I always will, no matter what happens. If you win that race, we lose. Don't let that happen. Please, Jesse, I love you!" He smiled at her and they kissed again.

The-crowds were a bit confused yet full—of joy as they kept cheering-the famous couple on. Photographers from newspapers and magazines were snapping their cameras and aiming their video cameras at them. Then they remembered the crowds and began to thank them for their support in the race. The announcers, confused also cheered them and thanked them both for their part in the race. Jesse then asked Rodney secretly: "Did you know about this?" Rodney replied: "Know?! It was my idea!" Jesse said to Rodney: "It figures! And, by the way, Thanks!!"
It was a day to remember and one that would go down in history.

Chapter Thirteen

Now, the day for the grounds ceremony for Francie's Dance Therapy School was to begin. Jesse began to have those doubts or fears again about whether it was selfish on his part to continue with Francie. Maybe he should force himself to stay away from her. Maybe it would be better for Francie if he did "win that race" she told him not to. Rodney reading his mind said to Jesse: "Champ, don't even think about it!!! You won't be a champ if you do. This is one race you must lose to win!" Yet, stubborn Jesse still kept wondering what was the right thing to do. Dad noticed it too. So, he thought he better tell Jesse about the ceremony for Francie's school where he is supposed to be the surprise celebrity to give Francie her bouquet of roses and scissors to cut the ribbon. Jesse didn't know what to do, but Dad told him that it was too late to get anyone else to take his place, and besides no one ever could: So, he agreed, but he was worried as to what to do about Francie and him—about their relationship.

Then all of a sudden a news bulletin came on the air and they announced that Francie was in the hospital due to an accident she was in on her way to the grounds ceremony for her Dance Therapy School. It seemed that a car crashed into the car in which she was riding. Yet they reported that there no deaths or fatalities. Mom and Angie and Slippers were not with her at the time. Francie was supposed to meet them there at the grounds ceremony of the future dance school. She went early to help with some of the details she had to go over with the crew and the media people. 'Her chauffeur' was not badly hurt, bruises mainly. She was not badly hurt either it seemed but the doctors could not say due to her unconscious state. She had passed out and seemed to stay in that state longer than expected. She was rushed to Intensive Care.

Mom cried and yelled as she heard the news on the radio when she was fixing Angie's hair for the ceremony. Slippers calmed Angie, but Mom was very afraid. She rushed to the hospital with Angie and Slippers.

Jesse cried and yelled in agony when he heard the news on TV. "No! God! Please. no!!! Don't let her die. Please, take me instead!" Dad and Rodney tried to comfort-him, but they were not successful. They rushed over to the hospital. the same ore where Francie had been operated on before. Dad hugged Mom who was crying desperately, trying to offer her hope and support. Jesse couldn't stand the waiting, so he went to the chapel to pray, where they had prayed before during Francie's operation there at the hospital. Dad and Mom followed with Angie and Slippers. They all joined hands and prayed for Francie together. Mom took out the rosary Francie had given her one Mother's Day. She remembered the Virgin Mary's statue with the baby Jesus at the church, where she used to go to pray for Francie before her operation and they used to light the candles for their prayers with Francie and Slippers. Then she closed her eyes and prayed to the Virgin Mary and Jesus and said: "Oh, Blessed Mother of God, Dear Mom, please answer my prayer for Francie again. Please save her. Please. If you can, take me instead. She is so young and so good. She wants to help others. Please help her to do so. Help her to live. Please, Mom. Please, Jesus. Please be with her whatever happens. Help me to accept Thy Will," she said when she saw the cross in the chapel, "yet, please, save Francie. Please."

Jesse also prayed, saying: "Forgive me, Lord, for I have been selfish and even jealous of Francie being able to walk and those around her who could dance with her like I could not, and do all of the things that I wish I could share with her.

49

I am not selfish anymore, Lord. I realize now that I love her and will always love her no matter what shape she may be in, wheels or no wheels. I'd rather die than lose her forever. Oh, Lord, forgive me. I know Thy Will be done. Yet, please, take me instead. I'm not as good and pure as she is. All she wants to do is to love purely and truly from the heart, always thinking of others and reaching out to those in need. Oh, please, don't take her now for their sakes and mine—I need her, too, and now I know that nothing else matters, except for love. I love her, Lord. I promise to love her always. This time I really will love her for always and never let her go. I won't be a coward and run away like before. Maybe I did run away, because I love her, thinking that it was best for her. I really thought it was best for her, so maybe I wasn't completely selfish. Yet, I was wrong in staying away from her and trying to run away again. I know that now, because the love I feel for her cannot die. It is a gift from You, Lord, to both Francie and me. To try to kill it is wrong; to run away from it is also wrong. When love is true it is meant to be shared. I know now that it may be too late. Oh, Lord, I've always loved Francie, and I always will. That is all that really matters, Lord–love is all that matters. The rest can be dealt with if one has love. I've been a fool to wait to realize this for so long now. I've made a mess of things even trying to do what I felt was right. How blind can I be?! I Please, save her if it is Thy Will. I promise this time to share my love with her forever. I'll never run from it again. Oh, please, Lord, give me another chance. Now, I know what Rodney meant when he said, 'It is the dance in your heart that is the only true and best dance of all.' This is why Francie still loved me even after she could dance ballet and was free of me or so I thought. I couldn't see that. I was too blind to see. I was even going to run away again not believing this could be so. Forgive me, Lord, please. Forgive me. I believe now. I believe in our love. It's stronger than anything, because You gave it to us, Dear Lord. Francie never doubted, but I did. I was afraid and wrong. Trying to help her, I hurt Francie instead. Oh, Lord, please give me another chance to love Francie like she deserves, from the heart, without malice or jealousy or doubt. Oh, Lord, please give me another chance to love her again. .I promise, if it is Thy Will, that this time I will share all of my love with. Francie without doubts. I'll never run again. Help me to lose this race, so that I may win, like Rodney told me and also Francie the day of the Race. Please, Lord, win this race for France, for Francie and me. She's racing for-her life; I love her so. I need her so. How I wish I could tell her so. Please, Lord, I'll do whatever you want me to do, I promise. But, please save her. Please, and tell her that I love her."

Angie also prayed for her big sister and so did Rodney and Slippers. They all prayed for Francie. Mom and Dad continued to pray too.

Then all of a sudden the doctor appeared at the door of the chapel. He called Mom over and said: "Don't worry. It's as if a miracle. She's come to. We didn't think she would make it for awhile there, yet she's come to. We can't explain it. It must be a miracle."

Mom replied: "It is, doctor, it is. Thank God!"

Mom went back to tell the others. They all rejoiced* and gave thanks that their prayers had been answered. Mom said to the Virgin Mary and Jesus: "Thank you, Mom. Thank you, Jesus." Jesse also gave special thanks by saying: "'Thank you, Lord. I love you." They all hugged each other and gave thanks at the chapel. then they went to be with Francie. The doctor said: "Only one at a time, just in case." Then the doctor said: "Who's Jesse? She seems to be calling out to someone." Jesse, grateful, believed that his doubts were being reassured at this even more. He believed it was a 'sign and hopefully the answer to his prayer on what to do, on what it was that God wanted for them. He thanked the Lord for this beautiful sign and said:, "I am Jesse, sir." The doctor said: "Come with me, son. I'll take you to her." So he went with Rodney.

There was Francie, like an angel. He took her hand and said: "It's me, Francie. It's me, my love. Everything is going to be all right now. I promise." Then he kissed her hand. She smiled and sighed saying: "I love you, Jesse." Jesse, with a tear in his eye, said: "I love you too, Francie. I love you too!" The doctor said: "Okay, that's enough for now. She must rest." Jesse then asked the doctor is she would be all right. The doctor told Jesse: "Yes, son', I believe she's going to be all right.

She kept calling your name when she came to. Yes, I think that she's going to be all right." Jesse thanked the Lord again. So . did Rodney.

The next day Francie was already herself again, so Jesse took a bouquet of roses to Francie with another vase that said: "I love you forever—always." It had a heart on it too. Then he gave her a teddy bear with a heart on it. It said: "Will you be mine?" She smiled and hugged Jesse, thanking him then he took her hand and kissed it an said. "Francie, I love you. Will you marry me?" Francie was amazed. She couldn't believe it could really be. She replied: "Oh, Jesse, if this is for real, of course I will!!!" He said to her: "Francie, it's for real this time and for always. I promise . . . that is if you still want

this fool . . ." Francie replied: "Oh, I do, I do! Oh, and you're not a fool! I love you, Jesse!" They both laughed and gave each other a kiss and a hug, then he slipped the ring on her finger. Rodney was thrilled with joy.

Mom and Dad and Slippers and Angie all heard the good news and congratulated them. Rodney told Slippers: "Yes, miracles do happen!" Slippers said: "Amen!"

The doctor came in and congratulated them when he heard the news. He also told them that Francie was a very lucky young lady. He explained that it was lucky that she had been riding in-the front seat of the car instead of the back seat, where she would have sat had it not been for all of the things that she had put on the back seat of the car for the opening. The doctor explained that she would not have survived probably if she had been sitting in the back seat, which did not have the extra protection of the front seat air bags. They all looked at each other and Jesse put his hand over Francie's hand and squeezed it tight as they all silently thanked the Blessed Mother and the Lord for saving Francie and protecting her always.

Then they asked about the chauffeur and the doctor replied that he was also going to be all right. Later they went to visit him giving him Francie's regards. Yet, before doing so, Rodney and Slippers looked at each other in amazement of it all and, with their thoughts, spoke to each other and reaffirmed their earlier commentary: "Miracles sure do happen!"

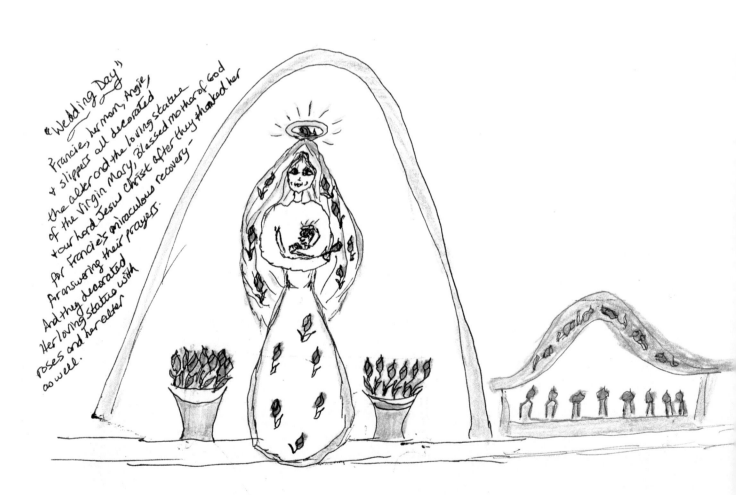

"Wedding Day"
Francie, her mom, Angie, & slippers all decorated the alter and the loving statue of the Virgin Mary, Blessed mother of God and the Lord Jesu christ after they thanked her for Francie's miraculous recovery— Answering their prayers. And they decorated Her loving statue with roses and her alter as well.

Chapter Fourteen

Francie was now well enough to leave the' hospital: The whole family attended the Grounds Ceremony for Francie's Dance Therapy School. There, it was also publicly announced that Jesse and Francie were engaged to be married very soon.

Then, the wedding day finally came. They were to be married at their parish church, Our Blessed Lady's Catholic Church, where Francie's mom and Jesse's dad had met after Mass that Sunday many years ago and where Francie's mom had prayed for Francie before she was able to walk again. Yes, this was a very special place for this family, which originally began here.

The statue of the Virgin Many and Jesus was surrounded by beautiful pink roses which Francie and her mom decorated personally with Angie's help too. Slippers lovingly watched. Francie's mom gave thanks to the Virgin Mary and Jesus for all of the wonderful miracles that they had blessed Francie and the family with. Francie, Angie, and Slippers also gave special thanks.

The altar looked beautiful also, filled with more pink roses just like the ones Rodney and Jesse had given Francie and Slippers the night that they met and danced with hearts and pink roses beautifully strung together that magical night in the family room.

Francie looked beautiful, more so than ever. Francie's mom designed her beautiful hair-do decorated with beautiful light pink roses that she wore as her crown, just like the ones at church. Her bouquet also had the same kind of roses.

Her veil came down out of the crown of pink roses. Her big brown eyes and golden brown hair looked beautiful. Her beautiful wedding gown had some small pink roses sprinkled on also. She looked precious.

Angie was the flower girl with small pink roses on her hair and a pretty light pink dress. Slippers was decorated with light pink roses too. Together they went down the aisle to the altar' where Mom and Jessie waited at the altar for Francie and Jesse's dad who gave her away to Jesse at the altar. Yet, before this they walked down the aisle towards the altar. When Jesse saw Francie he was overcome with love. He was so filled with love and joy that a tear came out of his eyes, especially when he heard their song, "The Magic Wheels of Love" which had been sung and played instead of the traditional Wedding March as Francie walked down the aisle towards the altar. Tears of joy came out of Rodney's eyes too. Jesse looked so handsome in his black tie and formal tuxedo. His dark shiny hair was styled just right. He also wore alight pink rose on his tuxedo. Mom looked very pretty too. All had tears of joy in their eyes as Dad gave Francie away to Jesse at the altar and throughout the lovely ceremony. When the priest said to Jesse: "You may now kiss the bride," Rodney and Slippers winked at each other as Francie and Jesse kissed. Mom and Dad followed the happy couple arm in arm down the aisle after the ceremony at the altar concluded. It was a beautiful wedding.

The wedding reception was also beautiful, and "The Magic Wheel of Love" song was also played at the party. It was their song forever.

The Wedding Song
"The Magic Wheels of Love"

And . . . guess who caught the bouquet? Yes, Mom did! And . . . guess who caught the garter? Yes, Dad did!

Rightly so, for they soon became engaged to be married. After Jesse and Francie came back from the honeymoon, they got married. They legally became Angie's parents through adoption, and Jesse and Francie, her legal guardians. Francie and Jesse lived in an attached home to Jesse's dad's home, which he built for them. Also, Dad's business became a success, and he went back to college and got his degree.

Jesse worked as a counselor and founder of the "Wheel Racers" with schools all over the world involved also. Francie, of course, taught dance and helped her students with her special Dance Therapy at her school.

Rodney and Slippers were alone for awhile conversing while the rest of the family was asleep and as they spoke remembering all of the wonderful things that had happened, they smiled at each other, and Rodney said: "It is so true what the Priest said in the wedding ceremony, when he said that Jesse and Francie's love for one another and all of the miraculous things that had happened to them is living proof that "with God all things are possible" and that Love is His greatest gift to all of us. Love passes the test(s) of time. Love endures forever. Love is the only true 'Magic'! After all, `The Magic Wheels of Love' keep spinning for you and me, for all of us, like .the song says."

Slippers responded: , "Amen to that! Amen! ! !"

The song, "The Magic Wheels of Love" now plays again as Rodney and Slippers remember the real life scenes of all that has happened to all of them since the very beginning, of all the wonderful loving miracles that they have all been blessed with so far.

Rodney and Slippers say to you (all of you) who are reading this (and/or) listening to this story: (Rodney speaks first) "Remember miracles air happen to you too! Keep your dreams alive always and believe, for `with God all things are possible.' Always remember: "The Magic Wheels of Love" keep spinning for you and me . . . for all of us!"

Slippers then adds: "Amen! ! !"

The End . . .

Or better said/written . . .

The Beginning

Printed in the United States
By Bookmasters